W9-AWP-562

RAND MᶜNALLY

Atlas
of AMERICAN HISTORY

Editor
Brett Gover

Cartography
Robert K. Argersinger
Gregory P. Babiak
Barbara Benstead
Marzee Eckhoff
Nina Lusterman
Rob Merrill
David Simmons

Design
Rand McNally Design

Photo Credit
Images provided by ©2000 PhotoDisc, Inc.

Copyright ©2005 by Rand McNally

Revised 2008 edition

All rights reserved. No part of this work may be reproduced or transmitted in any form or by any means electronic or mechanical, including photocopying and recording, or by any information storage or retrieval system except by permission of the publisher.

Printed in the United States of America

8 9 10 11 **BC** 09 08

Rand McNally
Skokie, Illinois 60076-8906

ISBN 528-93457-0

For information about ordering the *Atlas of American History* or the *Atlas of American History Teacher's Guide*, call 1-800-678-7263 (RAND), or visit our website at www.randmcnally.com/education.

Table of Contents

Introducing Atlas of American History

The features of *Atlas of American History* described below enhance understanding of America's past. They support and extend information from textbooks and primary sources. They provide additional links between history and geography.

Features of *Atlas of American History*

▲ Historical Maps
Maps are arranged chronologically. Each map includes a title that describes its content and dates that indicate the period of history it shows. Compare maps of the same area in different time periods to view historical changes.

▲ Map Legends and Labels
A map legend explains the colors and symbols used on a map. Historical maps often use solid or dashed lines to indicate routes of explorers or other groups of people. These routes may be labeled on the map. Labels also identify sites of historical events.

Captions
Each map has a caption that helps explain the content of the map. It may provide information about the historical context of the map or point out an important feature of the map. Legends, labels, and captions help tell the story of American history.

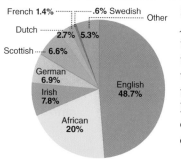

Population by National Origin, 1790

◄ Graphs
Some graphs in *Atlas of American History* illustrate information from the maps. Others provide additional information about American history. They may compare data or show changes over time.

Populations of United States Colonies and States, 1650-2000

States	1650	1700	1750	1770
Alabama				
Alaska				
Arizona				
Arkansas				
California				
Colorado				
Connecticut	4,139	25,970	111,280	183,881
Delaware	185	2,470	28,704	35,496

▲ Databank
The databank is a reference section on pages 72-75 of the atlas. It provides tables of information about the United States and its people.

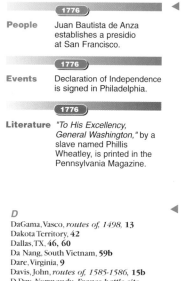

People — 1776 — Juan Bautista de Anza establishes a presidio at San Francisco.

Events — 1776 — Declaration of Independence is signed in Philadelphia.

Literature — 1776 — *"To His Excellency, General Washington,"* by a slave named Phillis Wheatley, is printed in the Pennsylvania Magazine.

D
DaGama, Vasco, *routes of, 1498,* 13
Dakota Territory, 42
Dallas, TX, 46, 60
Da Nang, South Vietnam, 59b
Dare, Virginia, 9
Davis, John, *routes of, 1585-1586,* 15b
D-Day, *Normandy, France battle site, 1944,* 57
Delaware, 21, 22a, 22b, 24a, 27a, 29a, 29b, 33a, 35a, 37, 41, 42, 43
Delaware (American Indians), 11, 35b
Demilitarized Zone (DMZ), Vietnam, 59b
Denver, CO, 46
DeSoto, Hernando, *route of, 1539-1542,* 14

◄ Chronologies
Each section of *Atlas of American History* includes a chronology. It lists people, events, and literature associated with the time period represented on the maps in that section. These listings provide connections that aid understanding of history.

◄ Index
The index is an alphabetical listing of the places and topics included in *Atlas of American History*. The index shows the page number(s) on which each entry appears. It provides explanatory information about many entries and refers to related entries when appropriate.

Periods of American History

Historians may divide American history into time periods in many different ways. Some periods may center around a theme, such as exploration. Others may center around an important event, such as the American Revolution.

Rand McNally *Atlas of American History* is divided into sections based on time periods described below. Some periods overlap to provide coverage of political and social history. Maps are organized chronologically within each section.

1. Beginnings (prehistory-1620)

Thousands of years ago, hunters from Asia migrated to the lands now called the Americas. These people, now referred to as American Indians or Native Americans, settled throughout the continents. They developed many different cultures, depending upon the environments in which they lived. They remained the only people in the Western Hemisphere until about A.D. 1000, when Vikings from Norway migrated to the coast of North America.

During the 1400s, European demand for Asian goods led Columbus to sail west across the Atlantic Ocean in search of a route to Asia. His discovery of a world previously unknown to Europeans touched off an age of exploration. During the 1500s, Europeans explored and claimed land in the Americas.

2. Establishing Colonies (1600-1775)

During the 1600s and early 1700s, Europeans came to the Americas for many different reasons. English settlers came seeking the freedom to worship as they pleased. Spaniards came to find gold and to spread Christianity. French trappers came to establish fur trade. Dutch settlers came for the promise of land. In addition, many Africans were brought to the Americas as slaves.

By the mid-1700s, English claims extended along the Atlantic coast, and the French controlled the vast interior of North America. Britain and France competed for control of the continent. As a result of the French and Indian War (1754-1763), Britain gained Canada and all of North America east of the Mississippi River.

3. Forming a New Nation (1775-1800)

English settlers in North America developed a prosperous economy and a way of life that differed from that in Great Britain. They began to resent Britain's control. They declared their independence and fought a revolution to win their freedom. As a result, the United States became an independent nation.

The original thirteen states stretched along the Atlantic coast. The western boundary of the new nation extended to the Mississippi River. Americans began to settle lands west of the Appalachian Mountains. The national government passed laws providing for the sale of western lands and the addition of new states.

4. The Nation Expands and Changes (1790-1870)

Much of the history of the United States is a story of westward movement. Between 1803 and 1848, the nation expanded its boundaries from the Mississippi River to the Pacific Coast. Pioneers had settled most of the land east of the Mississippi River by 1840.

	1769	1804	1933
People	Junípero Serra starts first Spanish mission in what is now California.	Meriwether Lewis and William Clark lead expedition from St. Louis to the Pacific Ocean.	President Franklin Roosevelt creates TVA to develop the natural resources of the Tennessee Valley
	about 700 B.C.	**1565**	**1787**
Events	The Adena (early North American Indians) build mounds in what is now Ohio.	Spaniards establish St. Augustine, FL, first permanent European settlement in what is now the United States.	Founders write the U.S. Constitution in Philadelphia, PA.
	1608	**1704**	**1868**
Literature	*A True Relation of Occurrences in Virginia*, by John Smith, describes the founding of Jamestown.	Sarah Kemble Knight's *Journal* describes the author's horseback journey from Boston to New York.	*Little Women*, by Louisa May Alcott, tells the story of four sisters growing up in New England in the mid-1800s.

In the early 1800s, fur trappers, traders, and miners pushed west of the Mississippi River, seeking economic opportunities. Soon they were followed by farmers and ranchers who settled the land. The promise of land and the hope of a better life also attracted millions of European immigrants to the United States.

5. A Nation Divided (1850-1865)

Different ways of life developed in the North and the South. Southern agriculture was based on slave labor. Industrial states in the North outlawed slavery. As settlers moved westward, new states were created. The question of whether to allow slavery in the new states led to conflict between the North and the South.

Debate and compromise failed to solve the problems. Eleven southern states withdrew from the Union. Between 1861 and 1865, the North and the South fought against each other in the Civil War.

6. Emerging as a Modern Nation (1860-1920)

Within 25 years after the Civil War ended, the process of settling the United States from coast to coast was completed. The settlement of the West also brought an end to the Native American way of life. The federal government sent soldiers to stop uprisings and move Indians onto reservations.

As the United States became an industrial nation, people moved to cities to work in factories. Millions of European immigrants also came to the United States seeking jobs.

The nation acquired territories overseas and began to emerge as a modern nation. By fighting in World War I, the United States also proved that it had become a world power.

7. Challenges and Changes in the 20th Century (1920-1999)

A period of prosperity followed World War I. However, the stock market crash in 1929 plunged the nation into an economic depression that lasted throughout the 1930s. During those years, the actions of powerful dictators in Europe led to World War II.

The United States fought in World War II from 1941 to 1945. It emerged as the leader of the free world, and the Soviet Union emerged as the leader of the Communist world. During the following decades, the United States intervened in many parts of the world to stop the spread of Communism. The Cold War finally ended in 1991.

8. Entering a New Millennium (2000 and beyond)

The United States has compiled information about the American population every ten years since 1790, when the first census was taken. According to the 2000 census, more than three-fourths of the country's 280 million people lived in cities. Americans born in 2000 could expect to live longer than any previous generation. Although many Americans lived in poverty in 2000, the United States had one of the world's highest standards of living.

The United States faces many challenges as it enters a new millennium. It must meet the needs of its diverse population. It must also continue its role of leadership in a rapidly changing world. The story of America is ongoing because today's events will become tomorrow's history.

1955	1969	2001
Rosa Parks protests segregation in Montgomery, AL by refusing to give up bus seat to white passenger.	U.S. astronaut Neil Armstrong becomes first person to walk on the moon.	Colin Powell, son of Jamaican immigrants, becomes first African American to serve as U.S. Secretary of State.

1848	1941	1970
Discovery of gold in California brings settlers to the West.	Japanese bombing of Pearl Harbor, Hawaii, brings U.S. into World War II.	Americans participate in Earth Day, a nationwide demonstration of concern for the environment.

1932	1976	1999
Little House in the Big Woods, by Laura Ingalls Wilder, describes life in the Midwest in the 1870s and 1880s.	*Roots: The Saga of an American Family*, by Alex Haley, traces the author's ancestry back to the African slave trade.	*Daughter of Fortune*, by Isabel Allende, tells the story of a Chilean-born woman who interacts with British, American, and Chinese cultures in the 1800s.

Benefits of Using Rand McNally *Atlas of American History*

Events gain fuller meaning.

Knowing where events took place gives them fuller meaning and often explains causes and effects. For example, the map of the final campaign of the American Revolution, on page 27, shows how American and French forces trapped the British at Yorktown. It helps explain why Cornwallis surrendered.

Connections among events are clarified.

Through the visual power of historical maps, the links between and among events become clear. The maps on pages 12 and 13 show international trade routes, 1350-1450, and Portuguese routes to India in the 1400s. They help explain why Europeans wanted to find an all-water route to Asia. They provide the background to understanding the age of exploration that followed Columbus's discovery of the Americas.

Similarities and differences become apparent.

The maps in *Atlas of American History* provide an opportunity to compare and contrast places over time. Compare the map of North America in 1763, on page 23, with the map of North America in 1783 on page 28. These maps show the emergence of the United States on a continent claimed by Britain and Spain.

The maps in this atlas also provide an opportunity to compare and contrast regions of the United States. The map titled "A Quarreling People," on page 41, indicates differences between the North and the South at the time of the Civil War.

The influence of sense of place is conveyed.

Maps in *Atlas of American History* convey people's sense of place at a particular time in history. The map titled "Opportunities and Uncertainties," on page 58, is a good example. The map's polar projection emphasizes how near the Soviet Union is to the United States. It reflects Americans' fear of nuclear attack from the north during the postwar period of tension between the United States and the Soviet Union.

Trends emerge.

The maps in this atlas show trends in American history. The map of Westward Expansion, on pages 36-37, shows the sequence in which the United States acquired land. It indicates the westward movement of settlement patterns. The maps on pages 38, 48, and 61 indicate changing trends in immigration.

The story of American history is communicated.

The text in *Atlas of American History* presents a chronological overview of American history and summarizes key events. It provides cross curricular connections by listing literature that clarifies or expands historical understandings. It highlights people whose accomplishments reflect American ideals.

The *Did You Know?* feature on each section opening page provides an interesting sidelight to history. Like the example below, each of these features demonstrates how history has influenced the American experience.

A picture of the Greek god Atlas supporting the earth on his shoulders appeared on the title page of an early book of maps. Later, people began to call a collection of maps an *atlas*.

Section 1   *(Prehistory-1620)*

Beginnings

To learn about **prehistory**, or the time before human beings learned to write, scientists study the physical evidence that early people left behind. This evidence suggests the first Americans migrated from Asia between 25,000 and 8,000 years ago. The descendants of these people, now called Native Americans or American Indians, spread throughout the Americas and developed different cultures.

Historical evidence indicates that Vikings from Norway established a settlement in North America about A.D. 1000. During the 1400s, increased demand for Asian goods led European nations to seek a water route to Asia. Columbus was attempting to achieve this goal when he discovered a world previously unknown to Europeans.

During the 1500s, European explorers who came to the Americas found continents inhabited by native peoples of diverse cultures, from hunters and gatherers to advanced civilizations. Although figures vary greatly, the graph at the right indicates estimates of Native American populations around that time.

◀ The Cliff Palace in Mesa Verde, Colorado, was built by the Anasazi around 1100.

In 1524, Verrazano ▶ explored the Atlantic coast of what is now North Carolina.

Did You Know ?

Scientists discovered a spearhead among bones of ancient bison near Folsom, New Mexico. These animals became extinct about 10,000 years ago. This discovery proved people had migrated to the region by about 8000 B.C.

Estimates of Native American Populations in 1492

Region	Population in millions
North America	~4.5
Mexico	~21.5
Central America	~5.5
Caribbean	~6
Andes	~11.5
Lowland South America	~9

(0, 5, 10, 15, 20, 25 — Population in millions)

	about A.D. 1000	1492	1587
People	Leif Ericson establishes a Viking settlement on the east coast of North America.	Christopher Columbus lands on San Salvador.	Virginia Dare, first English child born in America, is born on Roanoke Island.
	about 23,000 B.C.	**1325**	**about 1570**
Events	First Americans probably migrate from Asia to North America.	Aztecs build Tenochtitlán on site of present-day Mexico City.	Five Indian tribes in what is now New York form League of the Iroquois.
	1298	**1504**	**1552**
Literature	*Description of the World*, by Marco Polo, tells of the Italian trader's journey from Venice to China.	*New World*, a letter by Amerigo Vespucci, becomes the basis for naming America.	*In Defense of the Indian*, by Bartolomé de Las Casas, criticizes the Spanish for abusing Indians on Hispaniola.

During the Ice Ages, much of Earth's water was frozen in glaciers. These huge ice sheets covered much of what is now Canada and the northern United States. Scientists believe a land bridge existed where the Bering Strait now separates Asia and Alaska. Between 25,000 and 10,000 years ago, people from Asia may have migrated across the land bridge and spread throughout North America and South America.

**Routes of the First Americans
23,000–8,000 B.C.**

0   200   400   800   1200   miles at equator

Known routes
Probable route
Extent of ice

a

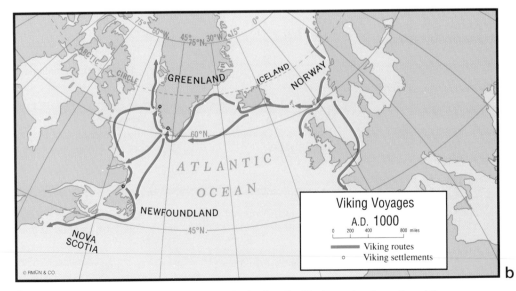

**Viking Voyages
A.D. 1000**

0   200   400   800   miles

Viking routes
○ Viking settlements

b

▲ About A.D. 1000, Norwegian Vikings, who had settled in Greenland, explored the coast of North America. They established a settlement in what is now Newfoundland, Canada.

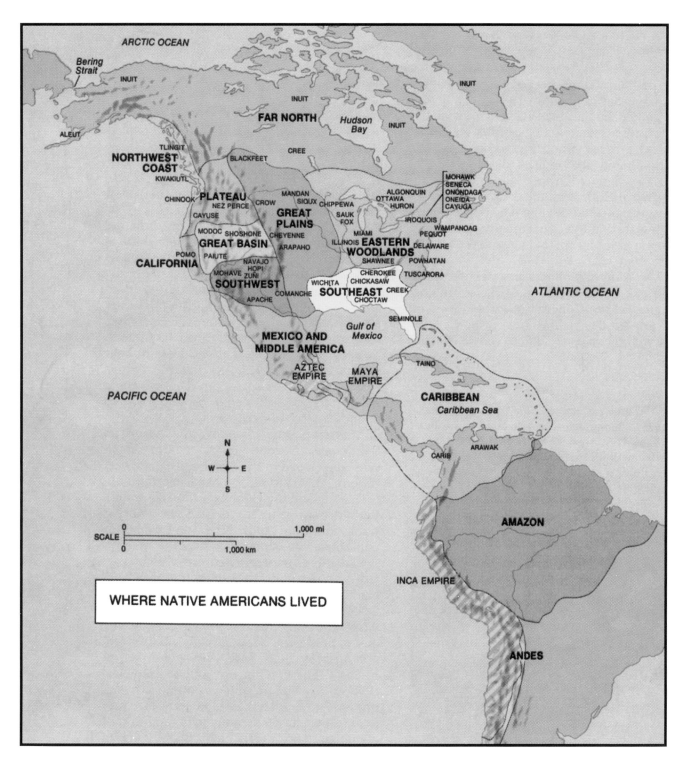

WHERE NATIVE AMERICANS LIVED

▲ Environments in which tribes of Native Americans or American Indians followed
a similar way of life are called culture areas. The culture areas shown on the
map existed around 1500, when Europeans began to arrive in the Americas. The
map also lists major tribes of Native Americans within each culture area.

From *America's Story* by Jacobs, Wilder, Ludlum, and Brown. Copyright © 1988 by Houghton Mifflin Company. All rights reserved.
Reprinted by permission of McDougal Littell, Inc., a division of Houghton Mifflin Company.

amber
flax
fur
hemp
honey
slaves
tallow
timber
wax
whalebone

copper
iron
tallow
timber

Novgorod
Tver
Moscow
Kazan

iron
copper
lead
silver
wine
textiles
coal

Lübeck

gold
iron
precio
horses
carpet
manuf

coal
textiles
tin

London

Antwerp

Paris

Kiev

Lemberg
(Lwow)

Azov
(Tana)

Saray

Astrakhan

*ATLANTIC
OCEAN*

Genoa
Venice

Moncastro
Kaffa

Black Sea

mercury
sugar
wine
wool

Marseilles

Barcelona

CORSICA

SARDINIA

Ragusa

Salonika

Istanbul
(Constantinople)

Trabzon

Darband
silk

Caspian Sea

Naples

Bursa

Lisbon
Seville
Granada

Palermo
SICILY

Tabriz

silk

Algiers Tunis

copper   iron

CRETE

Ayas

Famagusta
CYPRUS

Aleppo

Beirut
Acre

Damascus

Baghdad

Basra

Isfah

Oran

Fez

Tripoli   Barqa

Alexandria

Cairo

animals
carpets
copper
iron
manufactures
naphtha
paper
textiles

Marrakesh

Agadir

Ghadames

cotton
gold
ivory
salt
slaves

Marzuq

Qulzum

Taghaza

Ghat

Aydhab

Jidda
Mecca

Arawan

Timbuktu
Gao

Agadès

Bilma

El Fasher

Sawakin

Sennar

Sana'
Aden
Zeila

Shihr

Berbera

Gulf of Aden

Sokoto

Kano

Mogadishu

Equator

Malindi
Mombasa

ZANZIBAR

gold
ivory
precious wood
slaves

Kilwa

INTERNATIONAL TRADE
1350–1450

—— Major Sea Routes

—— Major Land Routes

Beijing   Principal Trade Centers

Mozambique

Quelimane

Sofala

MADAGASCAR

Portuguese Routes
to India
1488-1498

Between 1350 and 1450, Italian cities controlled trade through the Mediterranean, and Turkish Muslims controlled the main overland routes between Europe and Asia. Demand for Asian goods led European nations to seek a water route to Asia. The globe shows the routes of Portuguese explorers who accomplished this goal. In 1488 Bartholomeu Dias sailed around the southern tip of Africa. Ten years later, Vasco da Gama sailed around Africa to India.

Lisbon

INDIA

Calicut

EAST INDIES

Dias

De Gama

Qaraqorum

Beshbalik

Bukhara
Balasaghuk
Samarqand   Urumchi
Kashgar   Kucha   Hami
Balkh   Yarkand   Turfan   Anhsi
          Khotan

Beijing
(Khanbalik)

brocade
fine textiles
jade
rhubarb
silk
slaves

Harat
Kabul
Qandahar   Lahore
Multan
Delhi

carpets
copper
drugs
gold
indigo
iron
manufactures
precious stones
precious woods
textiles

Hangzhou

Zhangzhou
(Zaytun)

Kanbaya
Diu

Satgaon
Puri

Guangzhou
(Canton)

PACIFIC
OCEAN

Arabian
Sea

Dabhol

Bay
of
Bengal

Pegu

Panduranga

South
China
Sea

brocade
camphor
porcelain
satin
silk
sugar
taffeta
tea

PHILIPPINES

Calicut
Quilon

CEYLON

Kalah
(Kedah)

Pasai

ambergris
aromatics
cowries
drugs
indigo
ivory
precious stones
spices
textiles
tortoise shell

Malacca
SUMATRA

aromatics
drugs
gold
precious wood
spices
tin

Palembang

BORNEO

Equator 0°

JAVA

INDIAN OCEAN

The Spanish in
the Americas
1492-1542

0   500   1000 miles

© RMCN & CO.

▲ *The voyages of Christopher Columbus led other Europeans to explore the Americas.*
Pope Alexander VI established the Line of Demarcation to prevent disputes between
Spain and Portugal over lands their explorers claimed. The Spanish conquered
Indian empires in Mexico and Peru.

▲ John Cabot attempted to reach Asia by a northwest route across the Atlantic Ocean. In 1497 and 1498, Cabot explored the coasts of present-day Labrador, Newfoundland, and Cape Breton Island (Nova Scotia). His voyages gave England a claim to North America.

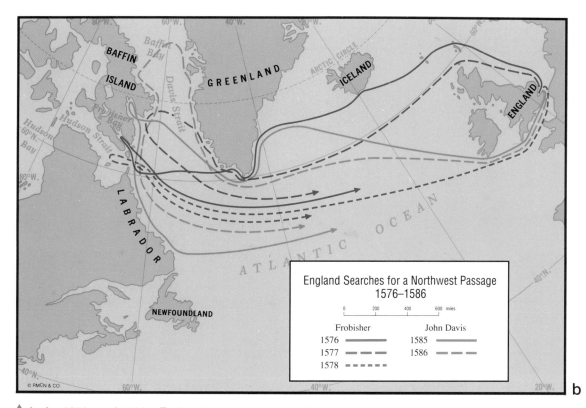

▲ In the 1570s and 1580s, England renewed its search for a water route to Asia through North America. Martin Frobisher and John Davis explored the Atlantic coast of what is now Canada and the area between Greenland and Baffin Island.

▲ France also sent explorers in search of a water route through North America. Giovanni da Verrazano explored the Atlantic coast from what is now North Carolina to Newfoundland. Jacques Cartier explored the St. Lawrence River and claimed the region for France.

▲ Samuel de Champlain extended French claims in North America. In 1608 he founded the city of Quebec. He then helped the Algonquin and Huron Indians defeat the Iroquois. Etienne Brulé lived among the Huron Indians and explored the river systems of northeastern North America for France.

Section 2   *(1600-1775)*

Establishing Colonies

Between 1600 and 1775, Europeans established **colonies**, or settlements ruled by their homelands, in North America. The English settled along the Atlantic coast and eventually took over Dutch and Swedish colonies established there. By 1732, thirteen English colonies stretched along the east coast of the present United States from New Hampshire to Georgia.

The French claimed the vast interior of North America. English attempts to settle west of the Appalachians led to conflict between France and Britain. The French and Indian War gave Britain control of all land east of the Mississippi River.

The colonial population grew rapidly due to a high birth rate and increased immigration. People came to America seeking religious freedom and economic opportunities. Slave traders also brought thousands of unwilling immigrants from Africa.

◄ This stone canopy stands near the Massachusetts shore. It covers Plymouth Rock, which marks the spot near which the Pilgrims are believed to have stepped ashore.

Reproductions of ► ships that brought the first settlers to Jamestown are on the James River in Virginia. They are near the site of the first permanent English settlement in America.

Growth of Colonial Population

Population in thousands / Year

Did You Know ?

Swedish settlers introduced log cabins in America. They built these houses along the Delaware River in the 1640s.

	1614	**1626**	**1682**
People	Pocahontas, daughter of Chief Powhatan, marries Jamestown colonist John Rolfe.	Peter Minuit purchases Manhattan Island from local Indians.	LaSalle claims Mississippi River Valley for France.

	1607	**1620**	**1754**
Events	Jamestown is founded.	Pilgrims settle Plymouth Colony.	French and Indian War begins at Fort Necessity.

	1640	**1650**	**1733**
Literature	The *Bay Psalm Book* is the first book written and published in the American colonies.	*The Tenth Muse Lately Sprung Up in America*, by Anne Bradstreet, describes home life in colonial New England.	*Poor Richard's Almanac*, by Ben Franklin, is published in Philadelphia.

English Land Grants
1606

0   50   100   150 miles

a

▲ *The Plymouth Company and the London Company were groups of stockholders within the Virginia Company. Each group obtained a land grant from the English king to establish a colony in America. Land between 38° and 41° north latitude was open to both groups. Neither group was allowed to settle within 100 miles of the other.*

The Dutch bought Manhattan Island from Native Americans and established a fortified trading center called New Amsterdam. They established other settlements along the Hudson River and later took over Swedish settlements along the Delaware River.
▼

Dutch and Swedish Settlements
1623–1643

0   25   50   75 miles

☐ • Dutch   ☐ ○ Swedish

b

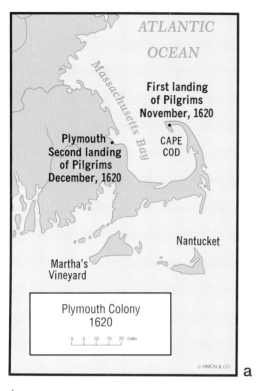

Plymouth Colony
1620

The Pilgrims named their colony
Plymouth, after the English port from
which they had sailed.

Early Settlements
in New England
1620–1630

In 1620 a group called the Council for
New England received a land grant from
the English king. The Massachusetts Bay
Colony was established on this land in
1628.

Expansion
of New England
1636–1640

The Puritans established settlements in
the eastern part of Massachusetts, shown
in blue on the map. Plymouth became
part of the Massachusetts Colony. People
who disagreed with Puritan views left
Massachusetts and established new
colonies.

HUDSON'S   BAY   COMPANY

L. Superior

Quebec

Montreal

Ft. Sault Ste Marie   *L. Nipissing*

Ottawa   JOLIET

Ft. La Présentation

Fort Frontenac 1673

Ft. Michilimackinac

L. Huron

Ft. Crown Point

Lake Champlain

Green Bay

Wisconsin R.

Fox R.

MARQUETTE-JOLIET

L. Michigan

LA SALLE

JOLIET

Ft. Rouillé

L. Ontario

Ft. Oswego

Ft. Niagara

IROQUOIS

LA SALLE

Mississippi R.

Ft. Pontchartrain (Detroit)

Ft. des Miamis

St. Joseph R.

L. Erie

Ft. Presqu'Isle

Ft. Le Boeuf

Ft. Venango

Hudson R.

R.

Ft. Sandusky

LA SALLE

Ft. Duquesne

Ft. Necessity

Monongahela R.

ENGLISH

Illinois R.

Ft. Crèvecoeur 1680

Ft. Vincennes

Ohio   R.

LA SALLE

Missouri R.

MARQUETTE-JOLIET

Kaskaskia

SHAWNEE

CHEROKEE

ATLANTIC OCEAN

Arkansas R.

Point reached 1673

Mississippi R.

CHICKASAW

Ft. Loudon

Ft. Prince George

CREEKS

Red R.

Alabama R.

Ft. Toulouse

French Influence in North America 1682

■ French   □ English

0   50   100   200 miles

Natchez

SPANISH

Biloxi

New Orleans

Cross erected 1682

GULF   OF   MEXICO

RMcN & CO.

▲ *France claimed the vast interior of North America, but it had little control over the region because of a lack of settlers.*

The Thirteen Original British Colonies, 1750

0   200   400 Miles

Copyright by Rand McNally & Company. Made in U.S.A.

▲ *In about 150 years, the British established the 13 colonies that would become the United States. By 1750 the British colonies had a population of more than 1 million.*

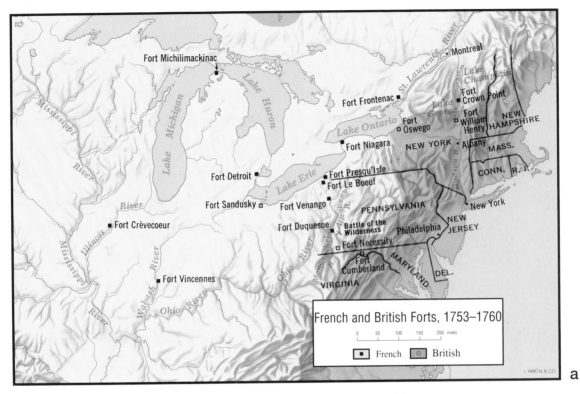

French and British Forts, 1753–1760

0   50   100   150   200 miles

■ French   □ British

▲ *To keep the British east of the Appalachians, the French built a string of forts from Lake Erie to the Ohio River.*

British Strategy in the French and Indian War 1754–1763

0   50   100   150 miles

— British campaigns

French   British   Disputed

▲ *The British captured French forts in the St. Lawrence Valley and the eastern Great Lakes region.*

The following labels appear on the map:

ENGLISH

UNEXPLORED

LOUISIANA

SPANISH

BOUNDARY CLAIMED BY HUDSON'S BAY COMPANY

QUEBEC PROVINCE

St. Lawrence R.

LINE OF PROCLAMATION OF 1763

L. Superior
L. Michigan
L. Huron
L. Erie
L. Ontario

Mississippi

Rio Grande

NEWFOUNDLAND
MIQUELON (FR.)
ST. PIERRE (FR.)

ATLANTIC OCEAN

PACIFIC OCEAN

GULF OF MEXICO

TROPIC OF CANCER

CUBA (SP.)

JAMAICA (ENG.)

HISPANIOLA
HAITI (FR.)
Santo Domingo (SP.)

PUERTO RICO (SP.)

GUADELOUPE (FR.)

DOMINICA (ENG.)
MARTINIQUE (FR.)
ST. VINCENT (ENG.)
GRENADA (ENG.)
TOBAGO (ENG.)

CARIBBEAN SEA

110°W. 100°W. 90°W. 80°W. 70°W. 60°W. 50°W.
40°N. 30°N. 20°N. 10°N.

**North America
1763**

0   100   200   400   600 miles

Spanish   English   French

© RMCN & CO.

The French and Indian War ended French control in North America. According to the Treaty of Paris in 1763, France kept only a few islands in the Caribbean. Britain acquired Canada and all French lands east of the Mississippi River. From Spain, France's ally in the war, Britain acquired Florida. To make up for the loss of Florida, France gave Spain the vast land between the Mississippi River and the Rocky Mountains.

Sources of Wealth in the British Colonies 1770

0   100   200 miles

- Needle-leaved forests
- Broad-leaved forests
- Mixed forests
- Fishing areas

Ironworks   W Wheat
Shipbuilding   T Tobacco
Whaling ports   I Indigo
Naval stores   R Rice

GRAND BANKS

ATLANTIC OCEAN

PART OF MASSACHUSETTS

NEW HAMPSHIRE

Portsmouth
Salem
Boston Provincetown
MASS. New Bedford
CONN. R.I.

NEW YORK

New York
NEW JERSEY
PENNSYLVANIA Philadelphia
Valley Forge

MD.
Baltimore DEL.

VIRGINIA Jamestown
Norfolk

NORTH CAROLINA

Wilmington

SOUTH CAROLINA

Charleston

GEORGIA Savannah

© RMCN & CO

a

Triangular Trade Routes about 1770

0   500   1000 miles

NORTH AMERICA

English Colonies

manufactured goods

sugar, molasses
grain
livestock

sugar, molasses

rum

WEST INDIES

slaves (Middle Passage)

ATLANTIC OCEAN

GREAT BRITAIN

EUROPE

AFRICA

GOLD COAST

SOUTH AMERICA

b

▲ Some colonial trade involved the exchange of goods for slaves. Thousands of unwilling immigrants from Africa suffered terribly during the voyage to America.

Section 3 — (1775-1800)

Forming a New Nation

Between 1775 and 1800, the United States became an independent nation and established a new government. The Revolutionary War began when American minutemen clashed with British soldiers at Lexington and Concord in 1775. It ended in 1781 when Washington's troops, aided by French forces, defeated Cornwallis and his British troops at Yorktown.

The Treaty of Paris of 1783 recognized the independence of the United States and established its borders. The nation extended from the Atlantic Coast to the Mississippi River. The new states **ceded**, or gave up, their western lands to the federal government. The government created the Northwest Territory and provided for the sale of land to settlers.

The Constitution, ratified in 1788, established the government that remains in effect today. The census in 1790 indicated the national origins of the American population.

This statue in Boston honors Paul Revere's historic ride on April 18, 1775. Revere rode from Boston to Lexington to warn colonists that the British were coming. During the 1700s,

Spaniards built missions, like the one shown here, throughout the southwestern part of the present United States.

Population by National Origin, 1790

French **1.4%** · · · · · · · · · · · · · · · **.6%** Swedish · · · · · · · Other

Dutch · · · · · · **2.7%** **5.3%**

Scottish · · · · · **6.6%**

German **6.9%**

Irish **7.8%**

African **20%**

English **48.7%**

Did You Know ?

The states carved from the Northwest Territory might be different if Thomas Jefferson had named them. He suggested such names as Dolypotamia, Assinisippia, and Metropotamia.

	1776	1789	1791
People	Juan Bautista de Anza establishes a presidio at San Francisco.	George Washington takes presidential oath of office in New York.	Benjamin Banneker, an African American surveyor, helps plan Washington, D.C.

	1776	1785	1800
Events	Declaration of Independence is signed in Philadelphia.	Land Ordinance provides plan for sale of land in the Northwest Territory.	Washington, D.C. becomes the national capital.

	1776	1782	1787
Literature	"To His Excellency, General Washington," by a slave named Phillis Wheatley, is printed in the Pennsylvania Magazine.	*Letters from an American Farmer*, by Jean de Crèvecoeur, describes social customs in the United States.	*The Federalist*, by Hamilton, Madison, and Jay, urges New York to ratify the Constitution.

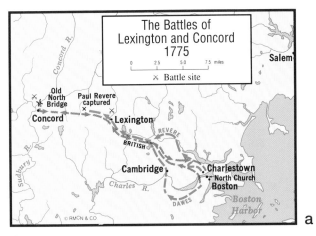

▲ On the way to Concord, the British were met at Lexington by minutemen who had been warned by William Dawes and Paul Revere.

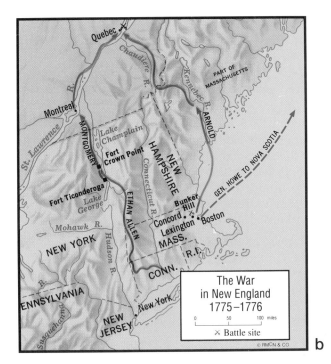

▲ Americans captured British artillery at Forts Ticonderoga and Crown Point. They used the cannons in Boston, where they forced General William Howe and his troops to leave. An American invasion of Canada, led by General Richard Montgomery and Benedict Arnold, failed.

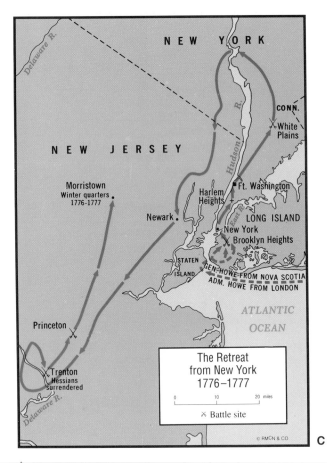

▲ The British victory on Long Island forced George Washington and his troops to retreat from New York. After victories at Trenton and Princeton, American troops moved to winter quarters at Morristown.

▲ Troops led by George Rogers Clark captured British settlements in the Ohio Valley.

The War in the South
1780–1781

0   50   100 miles

British   American
✕ Battle site

▲ British troops sailed to major ports in the South.

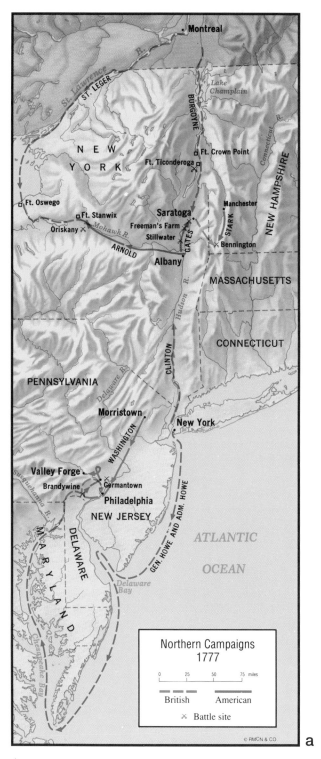

Northern Campaigns
1777

0   25   50   75 miles

British   American
✕ Battle site

a

▲ Americans suffered heavy losses at Philadelphia and Germantown, but their victory at Saratoga convinced France to enter the war on the American side.

The Final Campaign, 1781

0   10   20   40 miles

✕ Battle site

c

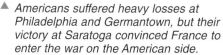

▲ The war ended at Yorktown when General Charles Cornwallis and his troops surrendered.

▲ The Treaty of Paris of 1783 established the boundaries of the United States. The new nation extended from the Atlantic Ocean to the Mississippi River and from 31° north latitude to the Canadian border. The treaty granted Florida to Spain.

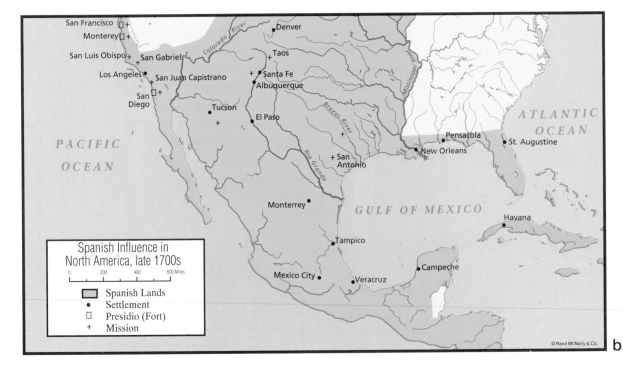

▲ Spaniards established forts to protect their lands and missions to spread their faith.

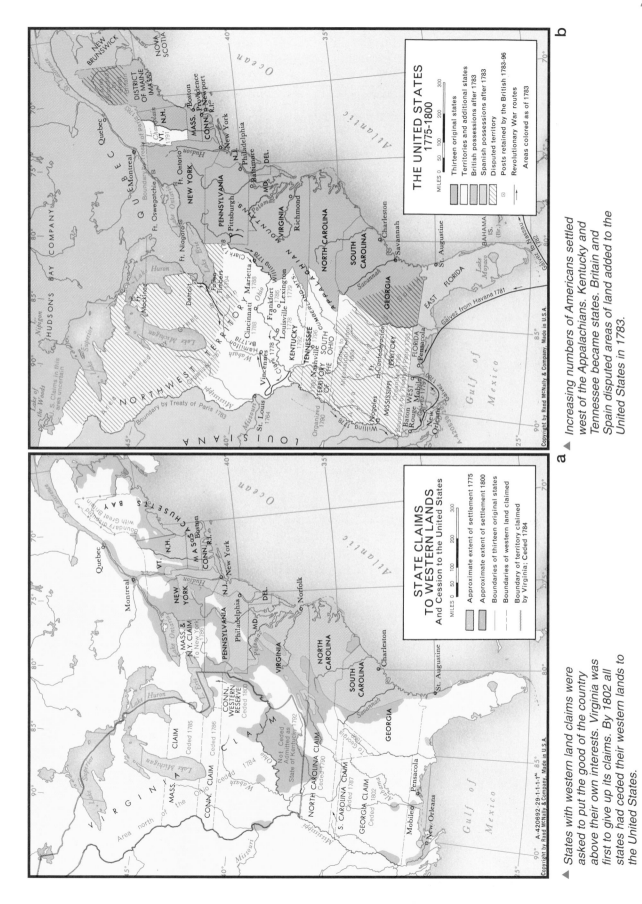

▲ Increasing numbers of Americans settled west of the Appalachians. Kentucky and Tennessee became states. Britain and Spain disputed areas of land added to the United States in 1783.

b

▲ States with western land claims were asked to put the good of the country above their own interests. Virginia was first to give up its claims. By 1802 all states had ceded their western lands to the United States.

a

Township

Section (640 acres)

The Northwest Territory was land north of the Ohio River that later became the states of Ohio, Indiana, Illinois, Michigan, and Wisconsin. The Land Ordinance of 1785 provided a plan for the sale of this land.

Public lands were divided into townships that were six miles square. Each township was divided into 36 sections, as shown on the diagram. Each section consisted of 640 acres, and it sold for $1 per acre. The small white square in the grid on the map represents one township.

In the 1780s, few settlers could afford to buy a section of land. Companies such as the Ohio Company and Scioto Company bought land from the government and divided it into smaller lots. Then they sold it to settlers at a profit.

Section 16 in each township was set aside by the government for the support of education. Settlers could rent or sell this land to raise money for public schools.

Section 4   (1790-1870)

The Nation Expands & Changes

Between 1790 and 1870, the United States expanded its boundaries to the Pacific Coast. Through the Louisiana Purchase in 1803, it acquired the vast land between the Mississippi River and the Rocky Mountains. Through war with Mexico, 1846-1848, it gained land in the Southwest. Through a treaty with Britain in 1846, it gained land in the Pacific Northwest. Within 70 years after the United States became an independent nation, it had tripled in size.

Explorers, trappers, and traders blazed trails to the West. Pioneers rapidly settled new territories, pushing the **frontier**, or edge of settled land, west of the Mississippi River. Settlers followed the Oregon Trail to the Pacific Northwest. Mormons traveled to Utah in search of religious freedom. Gold seekers poured into California. Millions of immigrants from Europe came to the United States seeking a better life.

◀ The Gateway Arch stands along the Mississippi River in St. Louis. It honors the Louisiana Purchase and the pioneers who settled the West.

This monument ▶ marks the Oregon Trail, which thousands of pioneers traveled from Independence, Missouri, to the Oregon country.

Did You Know ?

Francis Scott Key wrote "The Star-Spangled Banner" during the War of 1812 as he watched the bombardment of Fort McHenry from a ship in Baltimore Harbor. The words were set to music and later became our national anthem.

Area of Selected Lands Added to the United States, 1803-1867

1803	Louisiana Purchase	
1845	Texas Annexation	
1846	Oregon Treaty	
1848	Mexican Cession	
1867	Alaska Purchase	

0   200   400   600
Millions of acres

People

1803
President Thomas Jefferson purchases Louisiana Territory from France.

1847
Brigham Young leads Mormon migration from Illinois to the Great Salt Lake.

1848
Elizabeth Cady Stanton and Lucretia Mott hold women's rights convention in New York.

Events

1819
United States acquires Florida from Spain.

1825
Erie Canal links the Great Lakes and Atlantic Ocean.

1849
Gold rush brings thousands of people to California.

Literature

1820
"Rip Van Winkle," by Washington Irving, is set in the Catskill Mountains.

1827
The Prairie, by James Fenimore Cooper, describes frontier life on the western plains.

1854
Walden, by Henry David Thoreau, describes the beauty of nature in Massachusetts.

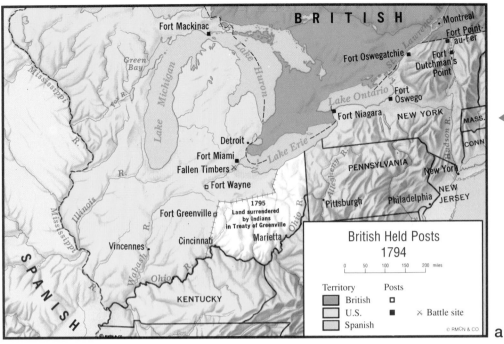

The British violated the Treaty of Paris of 1783 by keeping posts in U.S. territory.

Explorations of the Louisiana Purchase by Lewis and Clark and Pike provided valuable information about lands west of the Mississippi River.

Campaigns in the War of 1812 were widely scattered. They included a decisive U.S. victory on Lake Erie as well as the British capture and burning of Washington, D.C.

a

b

 The Treaty of Ghent set a boundary between U.S. and British lands and allowed both nations to settle the Oregon Country. The Adams-Onís Treaty set a boundary between U.S. and Spanish lands and gave Florida to the United States.

Routes to the West about 1840

0   100   200 miles

— Mormon Trail
— Fremont's Route
— Santa Fe Trail
— Oregon Trail
— California Trail

© RMCN & CO

a

◀ *The constant traffic of settlers to the Oregon Country marked a trail across the Great Plains and Rocky Mountains. Traders and trappers blazed other trails that settlers later followed to the Far West.*

The Mexican War 1846–1848

0   100   200 miles

✕ Battle site

© RMCN & CO

b

◀ *The Mexican War began with a dispute over the southern boundary of Texas—the area shown in pink on the map. It ended when General Winfield Scott defeated Santa Anna and captured Mexico City. As a result of this war, the United States gained a large territory in the southwest.*

The Removal of the Eastern Indians, 1840

The U.S. government forced Native Americans to leave their lands in the East and move to reservations in the West. The journey of 15,000 Cherokees from Georgia to Oklahoma became known as the Trail of Tears. About 4,000 Indians died along the way.

National Road and Canals about 1840

Roads
Canals

The Cumberland Road, also called the National Road, extended from Maryland to Illinois. The Erie Canal provided a link between the Great Lakes and the Atlantic Ocean.

WESTWARD EXPANSION
1800-1850

0 50 100 200 300 400

	U.S. Territory 1783
	Louisiana Purchase, 1803
	Texas, 1845
	Oregon Country
	Mexican Cession, 1848

IOWA
1846 States admitted 1800-1850
– – – Mexican War Campaigns
——— Western Trails
× Battles of Mexican War
+++ Railroads of 1850
▭▭▭ Major Canals of 1850

Between 1800 ▶
and 1850, the
United States
added fifteen
new states and
extended its
borders to the
Pacific Coast.

Copyright by Rand McNally & Company, Made in U.S.A.

◀ By 1850 settlement had spread west of the Mississippi River. Thousands of settlers also moved to the Far West.

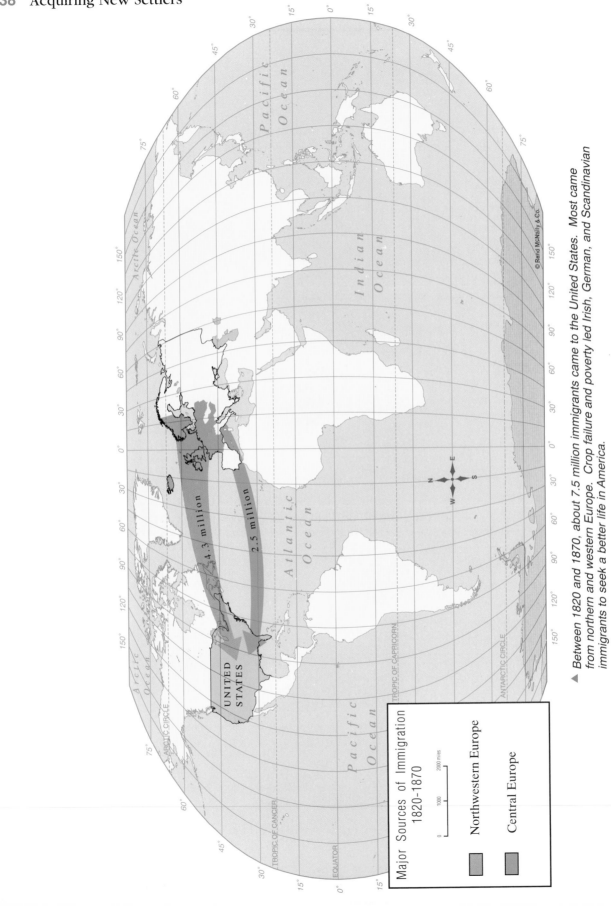

Major Sources of Immigration 1820–1870

Northwestern Europe

Central Europe

UNITED STATES

4.3 million

2.5 million

▲ Between 1820 and 1870, about 7.5 million immigrants came to the United States. Most came from northern and western Europe. Crop failure and poverty led Irish, German, and Scandinavian immigrants to seek a better life in America.

© Rand McNally & Co.

Section 5 — (1850-1865)

A Nation Divided

Between 1850 and 1860, differences between the North and the South widened. The agricultural economy of the South was based on slave labor. Many Northerners viewed slavery as wrong. **Abolitionists**, or people who demanded an end to slavery, operated the Underground Railroad to help slaves escape. The Compromise of 1850 and the Kansas-Nebraska Act attempted to settle the issue of slavery in the West.

When Abraham Lincoln was elected president in 1860, Southerners feared he would end slavery. Eleven southern states **seceded**, or withdrew, from the Union and formed the Confederacy. An attack on Fort Sumter in April 1861 marked the beginning of the Civil War. The war ended when Confederate general Robert E. Lee surrendered at Appomattox in April 1865.

The bitter war between the North and the South left lasting problems. Much of the South was destroyed. More Americans lost their lives in the Civil War than in any other war in which the United States has fought.

◀ The Battle of Gettysburg took place at this site in Pennsylvania in July 1863.

◀ This memorial to Confederate leaders is carved on Stone Mountain near Atlanta, Georgia.

American Deaths in Major Wars

- Civil War 618,000
- World War II 405,000
- Korean War 54,000
- Vietnam War 58,000
- Mexican War 13,000
- World War I 117,000

Did You Know ?

When Virginia seceded from the Union in 1861, 50 of its western counties separated from the state. These counties were admitted to the Union in 1863 as the state of West Virginia.

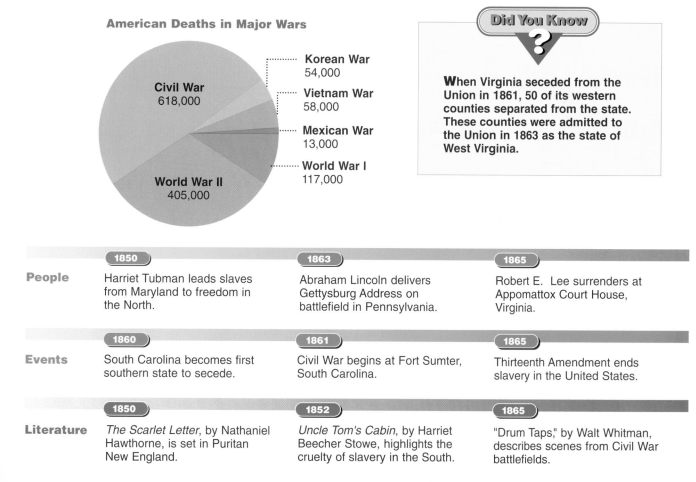

	1850	1863	1865
People	Harriet Tubman leads slaves from Maryland to freedom in the North.	Abraham Lincoln delivers Gettysburg Address on battlefield in Pennsylvania.	Robert E. Lee surrenders at Appomattox Court House, Virginia.

	1860	1861	1865
Events	South Carolina becomes first southern state to secede.	Civil War begins at Fort Sumter, South Carolina.	Thirteenth Amendment ends slavery in the United States.

	1850	1852	1865
Literature	*The Scarlet Letter*, by Nathaniel Hawthorne, is set in Puritan New England.	*Uncle Tom's Cabin*, by Harriet Beecher Stowe, highlights the cruelty of slavery in the South.	"Drum Taps," by Walt Whitman, describes scenes from Civil War battlefields.

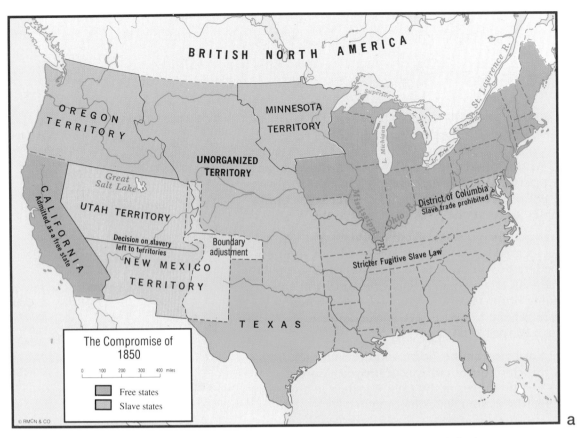

▲ The Compromise of 1850 admitted California as a free state and ended slave trade in the District of Columbia. Utah and New Mexico Territories could decide the issue of slavery.

▲ The Kansas-Nebraska Act allowed settlers in those territories to decide whether to allow slavery.

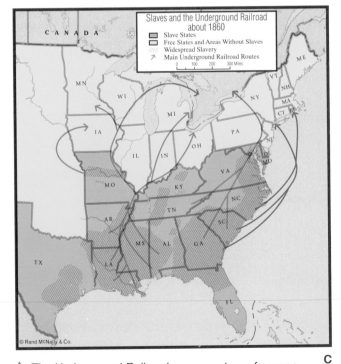

▲ The Underground Railroad was a system of escape routes slaves followed to freedom.

A Quarreling People
1820–1860

▲ *Economic differences created different ways of life in the North and the South. Plantation crops, such as tobacco, cotton, and sugar cane, supported an agricultural economy based on slavery in the South. Advances in mass production and transportation supported an economy based on industry and trade in the North. Northern abolitionists viewed slavery as wrong and began a movement to end it.*

▲ The Confederate States of America consisted of eleven slave states that seceded from the Union between December 20, 1860 and May 20, 1861. The 24 remaining states, including West Virginia (which split from Virginia and became a state in 1863) and four other slave states, fought for the Union during the Civil War.

43

▲ *Most of the fighting in the east took place in Virginia. Much of the fighting in the west took place in Tennessee and along the Mississippi River. The map legend indicates how Union strategy succeeded by dividing the Confederacy and blockading its ports.*

b 1861–1863

c 1864–1865

a

The Civil War 1861–1865

- ✳ Union victory
- ✴ Confederate victory
- ◎ Battle indecisive
- ↑ Union forces
- ↑ Confederate forces

Union strategy involved blockading southern ports, splitting the Confederacy by gaining control of the Mississippi River Valley, and capturing Richmond. Confederate strategy involved defending the South from attack, breaking the Union blockade, and splitting the Union by gaining control of Washington, D.C., Maryland, and central Pennsylvania.

Section 6 *(1860-1920)*

Emerging as a Modern Nation

The years between 1860 and 1920 included the end of one era in American history and the beginning of another. The Great Plains opened to settlers as the U.S. Army defeated the Plains Indians and forced them onto reservations. Texas cattle ranchers drove their herds to railroads, which provided transportation to eastern markets. **Homesteaders**, or settlers who received free land from the government in exchange for farming it, moved to western territories. By 1890, the long process of settling the United States from coast to coast was complete. The American frontier had come to an end.

In the late 1800s, the United States began to emerge as a modern nation. Millions of immigrants came from Europe to farm the land or work in factories. The United States became an industrial nation and acquired territories overseas. It purchased Alaska and established naval bases on islands in the Pacific. It fought a war with Spain by which it acquired additional territories. The United States entered World War I in 1917 and assumed its role as a world power.

◀ *This statue of Buffalo Bill Cody in Wyoming represents the Old West.*

The Statue of Liberty ▶ in New York Harbor has welcomed immigrants since 1886. It was a gift to the United States from France.

Immigration to the United States, 1860-1919

Period	
1860-1869	
1870-1879	
1880-1889	
1890-1899	
1900-1909	
1910-1919	

0 2 4 6 8
Millions of immigrants

Did You Know ?

In 1850 about 20 million bison, or buffaloes, roamed the Great Plains. The westward movement almost wiped out these animals. By 1890, only about 500 bison could be found in the West.

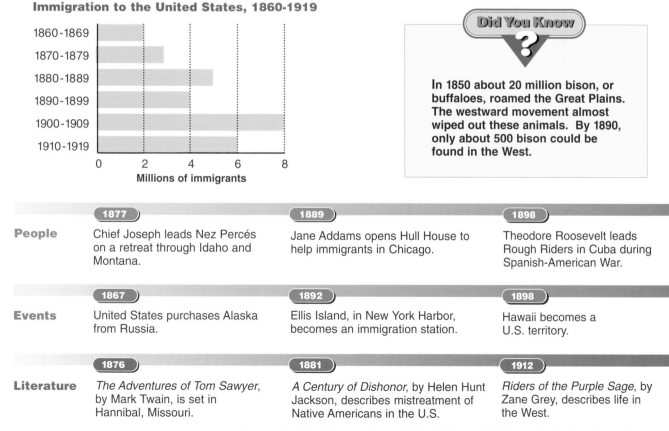

People

1877 Chief Joseph leads Nez Percés on a retreat through Idaho and Montana.

1889 Jane Addams opens Hull House to help immigrants in Chicago.

1898 Theodore Roosevelt leads Rough Riders in Cuba during Spanish-American War.

Events

1867 United States purchases Alaska from Russia.

1892 Ellis Island, in New York Harbor, becomes an immigration station.

1898 Hawaii becomes a U.S. territory.

Literature

1876 *The Adventures of Tom Sawyer,* by Mark Twain, is set in Hannibal, Missouri.

1881 *A Century of Dishonor,* by Helen Hunt Jackson, describes mistreatment of Native Americans in the U.S.

1912 *Riders of the Purple Sage,* by Zane Grey, describes life in the West.

Western Frontiers, 1860–1890

▲ *After 1860, the population west of the Mississippi River grew rapidly. Native Americans lost the battle to keep their lands, and the government moved them to reservations. Ranchers and farmers spread settlements throughout the Great Plains and the Far West. Although large areas of the West remained thinly populated, in 1890 the Census Bureau declared the frontier had come to an end.*

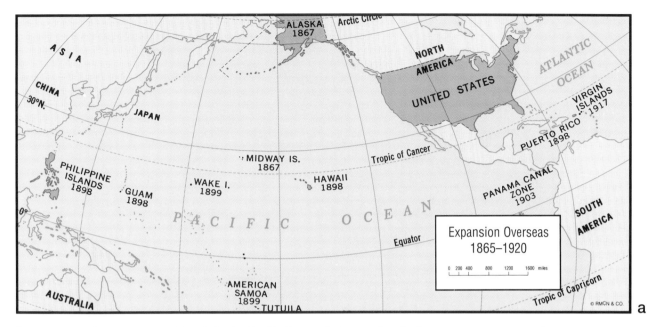

The United States acquired islands in the Pacific Ocean that served as fueling stations for ships traveling to and from China and Japan. The Hawaiian Islands also provided raw materials for import or trade.

The sinking of the American battleship Maine in Havana harbor brought the United States into war with Spain. The war was fought in both Cuba and the Philippines. As a result of the Spanish-American War, Spain granted freedom to Cuba and ceded Guam, Puerto Rico, and the Philippines to the United States.

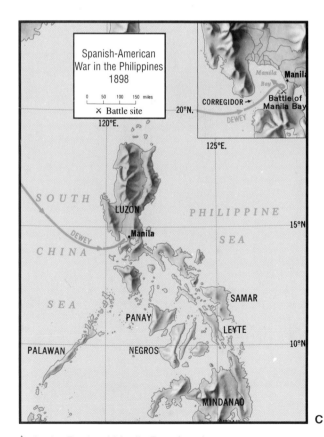

In the Battle of Manila Bay, American ships commanded by Commodore George Dewey destroyed the Spanish fleet in the Philippines.

Major Sources of Immigration 1880-1920

Northwestern Europe

Central Europe

Eastern and Southern Europe

UNITED STATES

6.1 million

6.7 million

8.1 million

▲ Between 1880 and 1920, more than 20 million immigrants came to the United States. Unlike earlier newcomers, who came mostly from northern and western Europe, these so-called "new immigrants" came mostly from central, eastern, and southern Europe.

Many immigrants settled in large cities in the East. Mining attracted newcomers to Montana, Colorado, and Nevada. Railroad companies encouraged European workers to settle in the West. Poor economic conditions in Mexico led thousands of immigrants to settle in the United States.

Immigration's Impact 1910

Foreign born and first generation Americans; by counties
(*Source*: U.S. Decennial Census, 1910)

- Less than 10%
- 10% to 25%
- 25% to 50%
- 50% to 75%
- 75% and over

0 100 200 300 400 miles

© RMCH & CO

▲ *In 1914, long-standing problems in Europe erupted in war between the Allied Powers and the Central Powers. The conflict, which became known as World War I, lasted four years. It involved more countries and caused more destruction than had any previous war.*

▲ *The loss of American lives aboard the* Lusitania *helped draw the United States into the war in Europe. American troops helped the Allies defeat the Germans on the Western Front, which stretched through Belgium and France.*

Section 7 *(1920-1999)*

Challenges & Changes in the 20th Century

During the decades between 1920 and 1999, the United States faced many challenges and experienced many changes. The economic prosperity of the 1920s ended with the stock market crash in 1929. Poverty and unemployment were widespread during the Great Depression of the 1930s. During World War II (1941-1945), United States troops fought in Europe and in the Pacific. After this war, the United States and the Soviet Union emerged as the world's leading powers.

The struggle between the Communist world, led by the Soviet Union, and the Democratic/Capitalist world, led by the United States, was called the **Cold War**. Between 1950 and 1990, the United States intervened in Korea, in Southeast Asia, and in Central America and the Caribbean to stop the spread of communism. The Cold War ended in 1991 when the Soviet Union was dissolved.

Changes took place within the United States as Americans moved from one area of the country to another, and suburbs grew around major cities. The **gross domestic product** (GDP), or value of all goods and services produced within the country, rose dramatically from the 1940s into the 1990s.

◀ *The United States Marine Corps Memorial in Arlington, Virginia, honors the flag raising on Iwo Jima during World War II.*

◀ *In 1940 Houston, Texas, ranked 21st in population among U.S. cities. By 1999, it was the nation's tenth largest metropolitan area.*

Gross Domestic Product, 1920-1999

Billions of dollars (Current dollars)
10,000
7,500
5,000
2,500
0
1920 1930 1940 1950 1960 1970 1980 1990 1999

Did You Know ?

Between 1941 and 1945, one in every five Americans moved from one part of the United States to another.

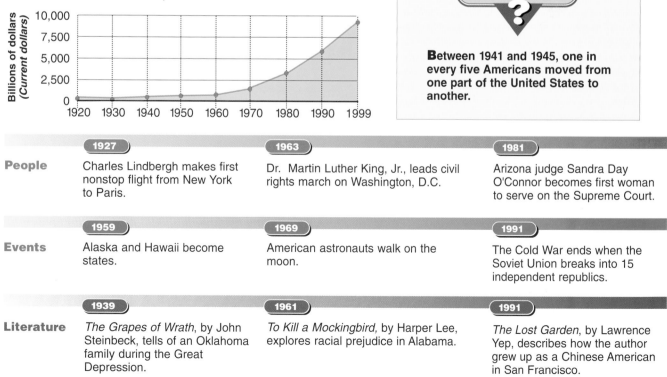

People	**1927** Charles Lindbergh makes first nonstop flight from New York to Paris.	**1963** Dr. Martin Luther King, Jr., leads civil rights march on Washington, D.C.	**1981** Arizona judge Sandra Day O'Connor becomes first woman to serve on the Supreme Court.
Events	**1959** Alaska and Hawaii become states.	**1969** American astronauts walk on the moon.	**1991** The Cold War ends when the Soviet Union breaks into 15 independent republics.
Literature	**1939** *The Grapes of Wrath*, by John Steinbeck, tells of an Oklahoma family during the Great Depression.	**1961** *To Kill a Mockingbird*, by Harper Lee, explores racial prejudice in Alabama.	**1991** *The Lost Garden*, by Lawrence Yep, describes how the author grew up as a Chinese American in San Francisco.

By 1920 the United States was a leading industrial nation. Advances in technology enabled workers to produce more goods faster. The demand for petroleum and steel increased to meet the growing needs of new industries such as the automobile industry. Spectacular economic growth provided a high standard of living for many Americans.

© Rand McNally & Co.

United States Industries, 1920

0 100 200 300 400 Miles

├─┼─┤	Main Railroads by 1920	▨ Textiles
⬭	Main coal deposits	⬤ Automobiles and ancillary industries
⬙	Iron ore fields	▲ Oil and gas
■	Centers of iron and steel production	

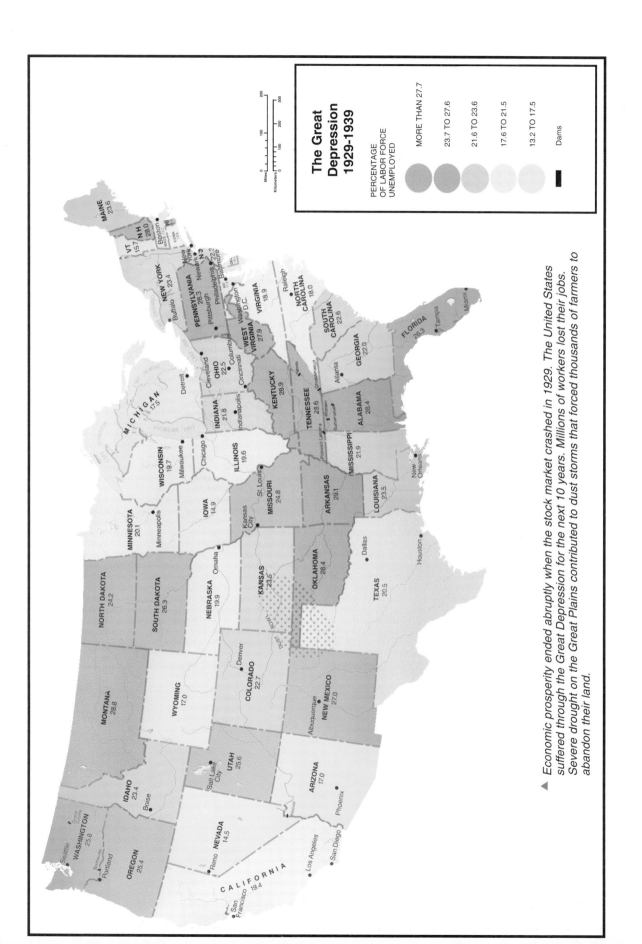

The Great Depression 1929-1939

PERCENTAGE
OF LABOR FORCE
UNEMPLOYED

MORE THAN 27.7

23.7 TO 27.6

21.6 TO 23.6

17.6 TO 21.5

13.2 TO 17.5

Dams

▲ *Economic prosperity ended abruptly when the stock market crashed in 1929. The United States suffered through the Great Depression for the next 10 years. Millions of workers lost their jobs. Severe drought on the Great Plains contributed to dust storms that forced thousands of farmers to abandon their land.*

MAINE 23.6
N H 26.0
VT 15.7
NEW YORK 23.4
PENNSYLVANIA 28.3
N J 22.2
WEST VIRGINIA 27.9
VIRGINIA 18.9
NORTH CAROLINA 18.0
SOUTH CAROLINA 22.6
GEORGIA 22.0
FLORIDA 26.3
OHIO 22.5
KENTUCKY 28.9
TENNESSEE 28.6
ALABAMA 28.4
MISSISSIPPI 21.9
INDIANA 21.8
MICHIGAN 17.5
WISCONSIN 19.7
ILLINOIS 19.6
MISSOURI 24.8
ARKANSAS 29.1
LOUISIANA 23.5
IOWA 14.9
MINNESOTA 20.1
NORTH DAKOTA 24.2
SOUTH DAKOTA 26.3
NEBRASKA 19.9
KANSAS 23.5
OKLAHOMA 28.4
TEXAS 20.5
MONTANA 28.8
WYOMING 17.0
COLORADO 22.7
NEW MEXICO 27.0
IDAHO 23.4
UTAH 25.6
ARIZONA 17.0
NEVADA 14.5
WASHINGTON 25.8
OREGON 25.4
CALIFORNIA 19.4

Seattle
Portland
San Francisco
Los Angeles
San Diego
Reno
Salt Lake City
Boise
Phoenix
Albuquerque
Denver
Omaha
Kansas City
Minneapolis
Milwaukee
Chicago
St. Louis
Dallas
Houston
New Orleans
Detroit
Cleveland
Cincinnati
Columbus
Pittsburgh
Indianapolis
Atlanta
Raleigh
Tampa
Miami
Buffalo
Philadelphia
Baltimore
Washington D.C.
New York
Boston
Newark

SOVIET UNION
(non-belligerent in Pacific War)

ALASKA

CHINA

Chungking   Shanghai

Karachi
INDIA
Calcutta
BURMA

Kunming

Hong Kong

Tokyo
JAPAN

PACIFIC

Dutch Harbor
ATTU
KISKA   ALEUTIAN IS.
9 days
12 days

San
Francis

MIDWAY IS.
✕ June 1942

8 days

WAKE I.

Pearl Harbor
Dec. 1941
✕
HAWAIIAN IS.

61 hours

PHILIPPINE IS.
To Japan
April 1942

GUAM

Prince of
Wales sunk
Dec. 1941
Singapore
To Japan
Feb. 1942

DUTCH EAST INDIES

CAROLINE IS.

MARSHALL IS.

OCEAN

INDIAN

OCEAN

Rabaul
SOLOMON IS.

GUADALCANAL
Aug. 1942
Coral Sea
✕
May
1942

26 days

NEW CALEDONIA

AUSTRALIA
Brisbane

Sydney

28 days

NEW ZEALAND

World War II
The Height of Axis Expansion
1942

Territory controlled by Axis
(Germany, Italy, Japan) late 1942

1941   Areas of German submarine concentration

Belligerents against Axis, late 1942. Also France, Poland,
Norway, Netherlands, Belgium, Luxembourg, Greece, Yugoslavia,
Philippine Commonwealth at war with Axis, before 1942.
North African and Latin American countries, 1943–1945.

✕   Battles

9 days   Days of ship time from the U.S.A.

20 hours   Hours of air time from the U.S.A.

Political boundaries as of 1938

▲ World War II began in 1939 when Germany, under Nazi dictator Adolf Hitler, invaded Poland. The Axis powers (Germany, Italy, Japan, and their partners) fought against the Allied powers (shown in gold on the map). Few nations remained neutral. By 1942 the Axis controlled most of Europe, northern Africa, and parts of Asia and the Pacific. German submarines attacked Allied cargo ships in the Atlantic.

The Japanese attack on Pearl Harbor, Hawaii, in December 1941 brought the United States into the war. American troops and supplies were sent to Europe and to the Pacific. The map indicates transportation time by air and by water from the United States to selected sites. During 1942, Allied forces halted Axis expansion in northern Africa, the Soviet Union, and the Pacific.

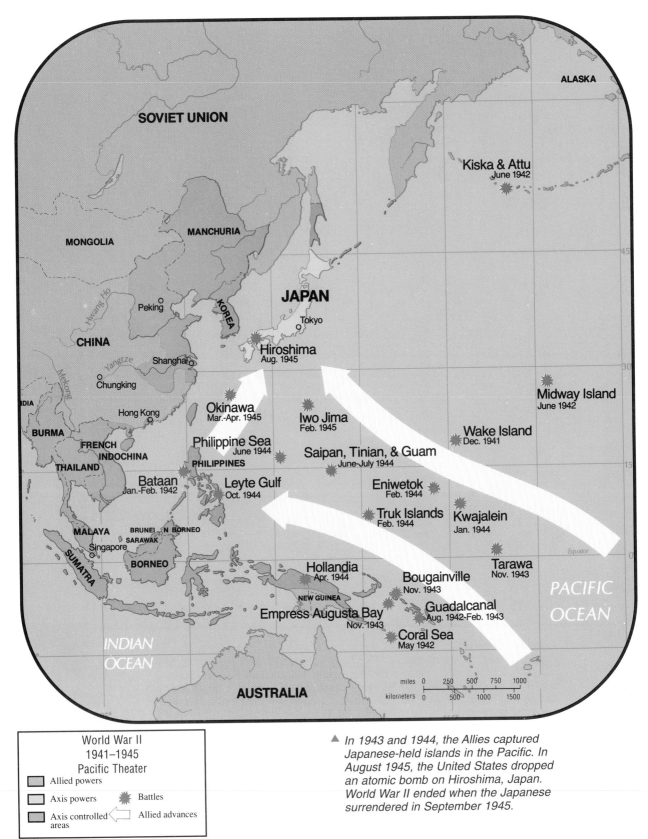

ALASKA

SOVIET UNION

Kiska & Attu
June 1942

MONGOLIA

MANCHURIA

CHINA

Peking

KOREA

JAPAN

Tokyo

Hwang Ho

Shanghai

Yangtze

Chungking

Mekong

Hiroshima
Aug. 1945

Midway Island
June 1942

IDIA

Hong Kong

Okinawa
Mar.-Apr. 1945

Iwo Jima
Feb. 1945

Wake Island
Dec. 1941

BURMA

FRENCH
INDOCHINA

Philippine Sea
June 1944

Saipan, Tinian, & Guam
June-July 1944

THAILAND

PHILIPPINES

Bataan
Jan.-Feb. 1942

Leyte Gulf
Oct. 1944

Eniwetok
Feb. 1944

MALAYA

BRUNEI   N BORNEO
SARAWAK

Singapore

SUMATRA

BORNEO

Truk Islands
Feb. 1944

Kwajalein
Jan. 1944

Tarawa
Nov. 1943

Equator

PACIFIC

OCEAN

Hollandia
Apr. 1944

Bougainville
Nov. 1943

NEW GUINEA

Empress Augusta Bay
Nov. 1943

Guadalcanal
Aug. 1942-Feb. 1943

INDIAN
OCEAN

Coral Sea
May 1942

miles 0   250   500   750   1000

kilometers 0   500   1000   1500

AUSTRALIA

World War II
1941–1945
Pacific Theater

- Allied powers
- Axis powers   Battles
- Axis controlled   Allied advances
  areas

▲ In 1943 and 1944, the Allies captured
Japanese-held islands in the Pacific. In
August 1945, the United States dropped
an atomic bomb on Hiroshima, Japan.
World War II ended when the Japanese
surrendered in September 1945.

World War II 1941–1945 European Theater

- ▢ Allied powers
- ▢ Axis powers
- ▢ Axis controlled areas
- ▢ Neutral nations
- ✴ Battles
- ⇦ Allied advances

▲ After defeating the Axis in northern Africa, the Allies focused on Europe. Italy surrendered in 1943. In 1944 Allies landed in northern France and advanced on Germany from the west, while Soviet troops advanced from the east. Germany surrendered in May 1945.

▲ In 1949 the United States and other free nations formed a military alliance called the North Atlantic Treaty Organization (NATO) to prevent the spread of communism. The Soviet Union and other communist countries formed a competing alliance called the Warsaw Pact. This view indicates why Canada and the United States feared a possible Soviet attack from the north.

Opportunities and Uncertainties
1957-1975

The Vietnam War 1957-1975

0   50   100   200 Miles

* Place of conflict

H-AA-H930X-AB- J-2-2
© Rand McNally & Co.

▲ The United States entered the longest war in its history to prevent communist-ruled North Vietnam from taking over non-communist South Vietnam. The Ho Chi Minh Trail was a system of roads the North Vietnamese used as a supply route for the Viet Cong, or communist rebels in South Vietnam.

b

The War in Korea 1950

0   50   100 miles

© RMCN & CO

▲ United Nations members, including the United States, sent troops to defend South Korea from an invasion by communist-ruled North Korea. In 1950, UN forces halted the North Korean advance at Pusan and pushed to the Yalu River in the north. The war ended in 1953 when the UN and North Korea signed an armistice agreement.

a

▲ Between 1940 and 1970, millions of African Americans moved out of the South. More than two-thirds of the total African American population relocated to cities. More than half the urban black population was concentrated in the twelve cities shown on the map.

African American Migration
1940-1970

Population Change due to Migration

Large population gain

Large population loss

■ City with large population gain

0   100   200   300   400 Miles

© Rand McNally & Co.

▲ Changes in U.S. immigration laws in the 1960s changed immigration patterns. Percentages of immigrants from Europe decreased. In the 1990s, most immigrants to the United States came from Mexico, the Philippines, Haiti, China, India, Vietnam, Jamaica, Cuba, and South Korea.

Major Sources of Immigration 1960s–1990s

- Asia, excluding the former Soviet Union
- Mexico
- Central and South America

0   1000   2000 miles

UNITED STATES

4.8 million

4.1 million

6.3 million

Atlantic Ocean

Arctic Ocean

Pacific Ocean

Indian Ocean

INTERNATIONAL DATE LINE

TROPIC OF CANCER

EQUATOR

TROPIC OF CAPRICORN

ARCTIC CIRCLE

ANTARCTIC CIRCLE

©Rand McNally & Co.

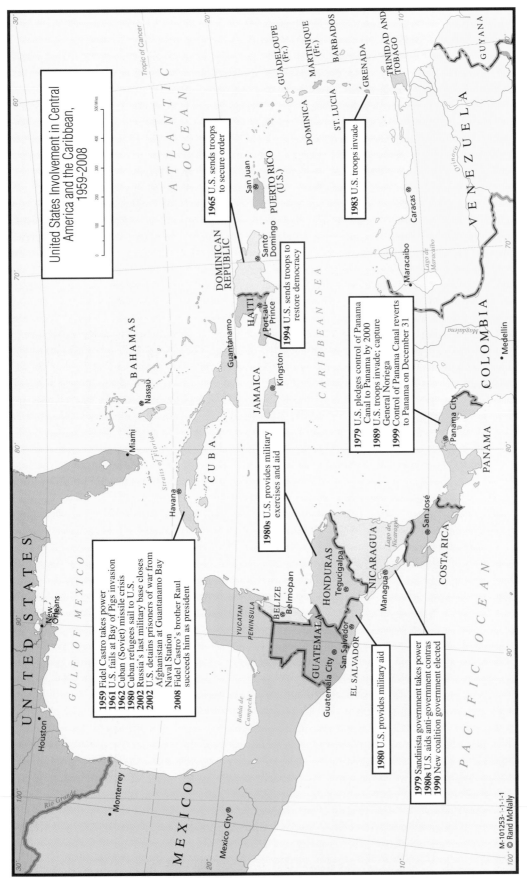

United States Involvement in Central America and the Caribbean, 1959–2008

ATLANTIC OCEAN

Tropic of Cancer

1965 U.S. sends troops to secure order

1983 U.S. troops invade

GUADELOUPE (Fr.)
MARTINIQUE (Fr.)
BARBADOS
DOMINICA
ST. LUCIA
GRENADA
TRINIDAD AND TOBAGO
GUYANA

San Juan
PUERTO RICO (U.S.)

Santo Domingo
DOMINICAN REPUBLIC

HAITI
Port-au-Prince

1994 U.S. sends troops to restore democracy

Guantánamo

CARIBBEAN SEA

Caracas

VENEZUELA

Maracaibo
Lago de Maracaibo

Orinoco

COLOMBIA

Medellín

Magdalena

1979 U.S. pledges control of Panama Canal to Panama by 2000
1989 U.S. troops invade; capture General Noriega
1999 Control of Panama Canal reverts to Panama on December 31

Panama City

PANAMA

BAHAMAS
Nassau

JAMAICA
Kingston

Miami

Straits of Florida

CUBA

Havana

1980s U.S. provides military exercises and aid

Lago de Nicaragua

San José
COSTA RICA

NICARAGUA
Managua

HONDURAS
Tegucigalpa

BELIZE
Belmopan

YUCATAN PENINSULA

GUATEMALA
Guatemala City

EL SALVADOR
San Salvador

1980 U.S. provides military aid

1979 Sandinista government takes power
1980s U.S. aids anti-government contras
1990 New coalition government elected

UNITED STATES

GULF OF MEXICO

New Orleans
Houston

Bahía de Campeche

MEXICO

Mexico City

Monterrey

Rio Grande

PACIFIC OCEAN

1959 Fidel Castro takes power
1961 U.S. fails at Bay of Pigs invasion
1962 Cuban (Soviet) missile crisis
1980 Cuban refugees sail to U.S.
2002 Russia's last military base closes
2002 U.S. detains prisoners of war from Afghanistan at Guantánamo Bay Naval Station
2008 Fidel Castro's brother Raul succeeds him as president

500 Miles
0 100 200 300 400

M-101253- -1-1-1
© Rand McNally

▲ *This map traces U.S. involvement in Central America and the Caribbean from 1959, the year that Fidel Castro took power in Cuba, to 2008, the year that he was succeeded by his brother Raul. During these five decades, the United States intervened frequently in the region to fight communism, support democracy, and protect U.S. interests.*

Section 8   *(2000 & beyond)*

Entering a New Millennium

In 2000 the United States was one of the world's leading nations. Its resources and technology made it a leader in the production of goods and services. Its principles of freedom and opportunity provided its people with one of the world's highest standards of living. The advent of the Internet had made it easy to exchange ideas and information quickly.

The diverse population of the United States reflected the history of a nation settled by people from every part of the world. According to the 2000 census, most Americans throughout the country lived in large **metropolitan areas**, or cities surrounded by suburbs. They earned more money and lived longer than Americans in the past. In spite of widespread prosperity, however, many Americans lived in poverty.

As the United States entered a new millennium, it faced new challenges in a changing world. Americans showed courage and resolve in response to terrorist attacks on New York City and Washington, D.C. on September 11, 2001. Defending human rights, supporting economic development, and protecting the environment have become global issues.

◀ *Skyscrapers tower over midtown Manhattan in New York – the largest U.S. city in population in 2000. Plans have been made for new buildings and a memorial park to replace the World Trade Center towers.*

Seattle, Washington, became an aerospace and technology center as well as a leading U.S. port for Pacific Rim trade. ▶

Did You Know ?

The Los Angeles metropolitan area has the largest concentration of immigrants in the country. Nearly one-third of its residents moved there from other countries.

Population Distribution by Age, 1900 and 2000

Age groups: 0-4, 5-14, 15-24, 25-34, 35-44, 45-54, 55-64, 65+

Percent of population: 5, 10, 15, 20, 25

	2001	2002	2007
People	Condeleeza Rice becomes the first woman and the first African American to be named National Security Advisor.	Ellen Ochoa, co-inventor of optical analysis systems and the first Hispanic female astronaut, makes her fourth voyage on the space shuttle.	Former vice president Al Gore receives the Nobel Peace Prize for his efforts to raise awareness about global warming.

	2001	2003	2008
Events	Terrorists attack the World Trade center and the Pentagon on September 11. In response, U.S.-led forces attack Afghanistan.	Scientists finish mapping the entire human genome, which contains the complete genetic formula for a human being.	NASA's robotic Phoenix spacecraft lands on Mars and begins collecting and analyzing soil samples.

	2000	2001	2002
Literature	*Interpreter of Maladies*, by Jhumpa Lahiri, wins a Pulitzer Prize for its stories about immigrants from India who come to the United States.	*Pleasure Dome*, a collection of poems by Yusef Komunyakaa, explores such topics as his Southern roots, his experiences in Vietnam, and jazz music.	*A Song Flung Up to Heaven*, by Maya Angelou, completes the autobiography of the African American poet.

United States

National Capitals

State Capitals

Cities

Urban Areas

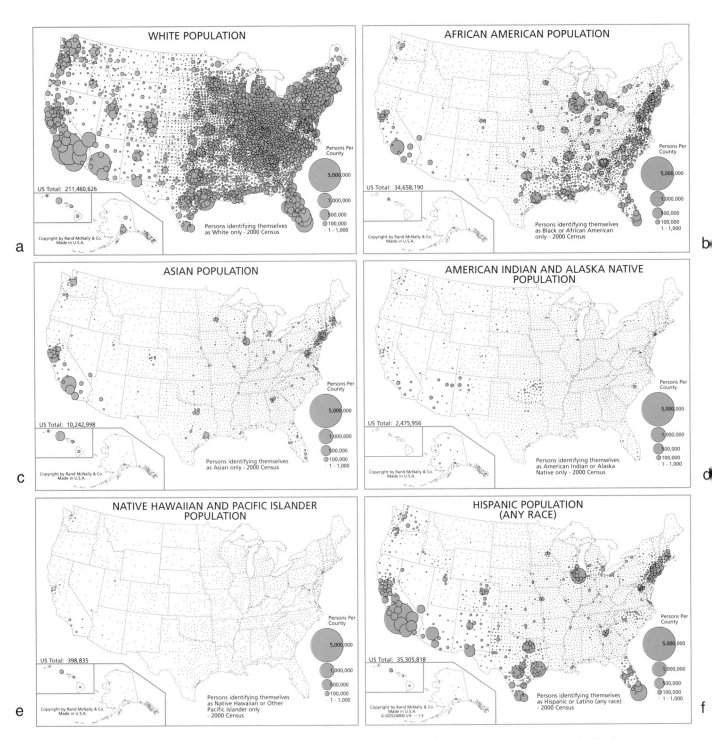

WHITE POPULATION

US Total: 211,460,626

Persons Per County

5,000,000
1,000,000
500,000
100,000
1 - 1,000

Persons identifying themselves as White only - 2000 Census

Copyright by Rand McNally & Co. Made in U.S.A.

a

AFRICAN AMERICAN POPULATION

US Total: 34,658,190

Persons Per County

5,000,000
1,000,000
500,000
100,000
1 - 1,000

Persons identifying themselves as Black or African American only - 2000 Census

Copyright by Rand McNally & Co. Made in U.S.A.

b

ASIAN POPULATION

US Total: 10,242,998

Persons Per County

5,000,000
1,000,000
500,000
100,000
1 - 1,000

Persons identifying themselves as Asian only - 2000 Census

Copyright by Rand McNally & Co. Made in U.S.A.

c

AMERICAN INDIAN AND ALASKA NATIVE POPULATION

US Total: 2,475,956

Persons Per County

5,000,000
1,000,000
500,000
100,000
1 - 1,000

Persons identifying themselves as American Indian or Alaska Native only - 2000 Census

d

NATIVE HAWAIIAN AND PACIFIC ISLANDER POPULATION

US Total: 398,835

Persons Per County

5,000,000
1,000,000
500,000
100,000
1 - 1,000

Persons identifying themselves as Native Hawaiian or Other Pacific Islander only - 2000 Census

Copyright by Rand McNally & Co. Made in U.S.A.

e

HISPANIC POPULATION (ANY RACE)

US Total: 35,305,818

Persons Per County

5,000,000
1,000,000
500,000
100,000
1 - 1,000

Persons identifying themselves as Hispanic or Latino (any race) - 2000 Census

Copyright by Rand McNally & Co. Made in U.S.A. A-GDS24000-V4- - -3-3

f

These maps show some major racial/ethnic groups in the United States in 2000 and where they lived.

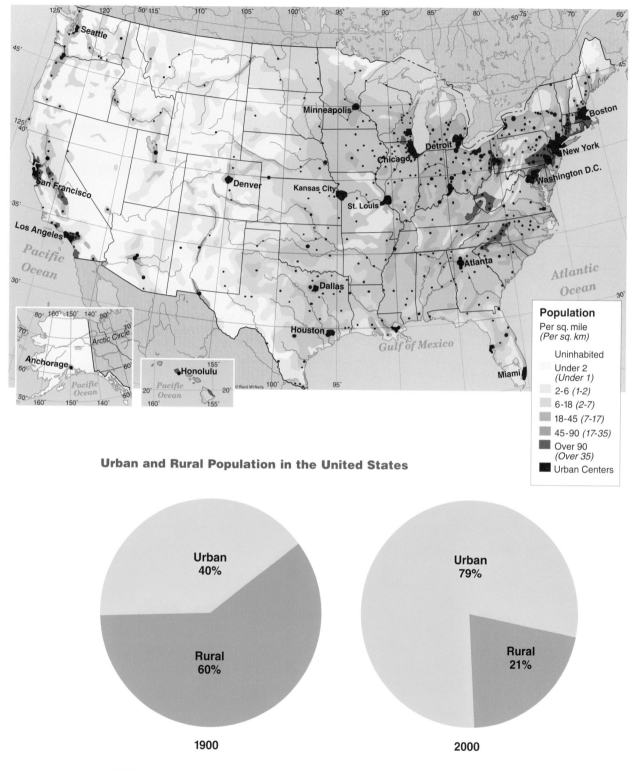

Urban and Rural Population in the United States

Population
Per sq. mile
(Per sq. km)

Uninhabited

Under 2
(Under 1)

2-6 (1-2)

6-18 (2-7)

18-45 (7-17)

45-90 (17-35)

Over 90
(Over 35)

Urban Centers

1900

Urban 40%

Rural 60%

2000

Urban 79%

Rural 21%

In 2000 more than three-fourths of all Americans lived in urban areas. The map shows the locations of the most densely populated parts of the United States. Notice that several metropolitan areas from Boston to Washington D.C. have grown together to form a large, densely populated area called a megalopolis. The circle graphs compare the percentages of urban and rural population in the United States in 1900 and 2000.

Median Family Income, 2000

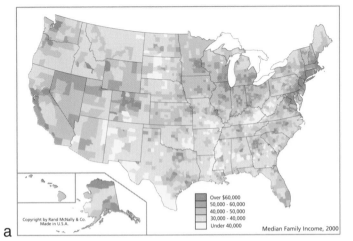

▲ The map shows median family income, or the middle value of all family incomes, in different parts of the United States in 2000.

High School Graduation, 2000

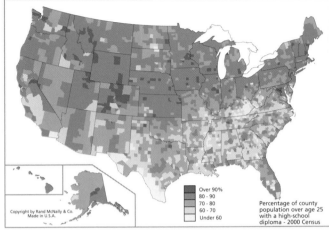

▲ The map shows the percent of people over age 25 who obtained a high school diploma in different parts of the United States in 2000.

Median Family Income (in current dollars), 1950-2000

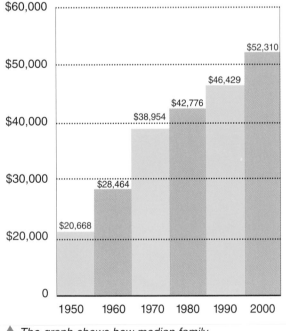

▲ The graph shows how median family income throughout the United States changed between 1950 and 2000.

High School Graduation Statistics 1940-2000

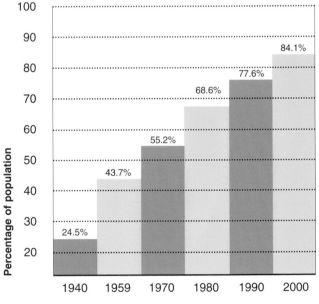

▲ The graph shows how the percentage of persons 25 years or older who obtained a high school diploma changed in the United States between 1940 and 2000.

Percentage of U.S. Population Below Poverty Level, 2000

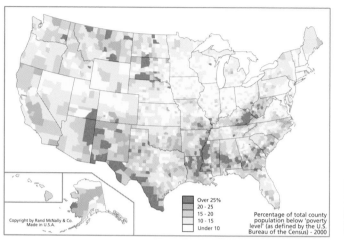

U.S. Unemployment Rates, 2000

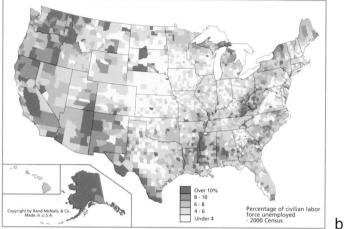

b

▲ The map shows the percentages of people living below the poverty level in different parts of the United States in 2000. Poverty level is based on the income needed to feed a family adequately without spending more than a third of the family income on food.

▲ The map shows the percentages of unemployed workers in different parts of the United States in 2000.

Percentage of U.S. Population Below Poverty Level, 1960-2000

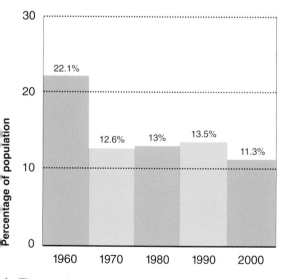

▲ The graph shows how the percentage of Americans below the poverty level changed between 1960 and 2000.

U.S. Unemployment Rates, 1960-2000

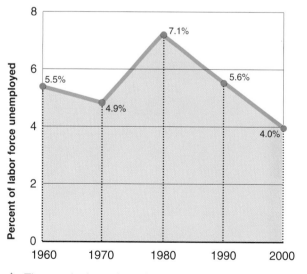

▲ The graph shows how the percentage of unemployed workers in the United States changed between 1960 and 2000.

The 50 states that make up the United States cover an area of more than 3½ million square miles. The United States is the world's third largest country in area.

In 2000 the United States had a population of about 280 million. It was the world's third largest country in population, smaller only than China and India.

Populations of United States Colonies and States, 1650-2000

States	1650	1700	1750	1770	1790	1800	1820	1840	1860
Alabama							127,901	590,756	964,201
Alaska									
Arizona									
Arkansas							14,273	97,574	435,450
California									379,994
Colorado									34,277
Connecticut	4,139	25,970	111,280	183,881	237,946	251,002	275,248	309,978	460,147
Delaware	185	2,470	28,704	35,496	59,096	64,273	72,749	78,085	112,216
District of Columbia						8,144	23,336	33,745	75,080
Florida								54,477	140,424
Georgia			5,200	23,375	82,548	162,686	340,989	691,392	1,057,286
Hawaii									
Idaho									
Illinois							55,211	476,183	1,711,951
Indiana						5,641	147,178	685,866	1,350,428
Iowa								43,112	674,913
Kansas									107,206
Kentucky				15,700	73,677	220,955	564,317	779,828	1,155,684
Louisiana							153,407	352,411	708,002
Maine[4]				31,257	96,540	151,719	298,335	501,793	628,279
Maryland	4,504	29,604	141,073	202,599	319,728	341,548	407,350	470,019	687,049
Massachusetts[4]	16,603	55,941	188,000	235,308	378,787	422,845	523,287	737,699	1,231,066
Michigan							8,896	212,267	749,113
Minnesota									172,023
Mississippi						8,850	75,448	375,651	791,305
Missouri							66,586	383,702	1,182,012
Montana									
Nebraska									28,841
Nevada									6,857
New Hampshire	1,305	4,958	27,505	62,396	141,885	183,858	244,161	284,574	326,073
New Jersey		14,010	71,393	117,431	184,139	211,149	277,575	373,306	672,035
New Mexico									93,516
New York	4,116	19,107	76,696	162,920	340,120	589,051	1,372,812	2,428,921	3,880,735
North Carolina		10,720	72,984	197,200	393,751	478,103	638,829	753,419	992,622
North Dakota[3]									
Ohio						45,365	581,434	1,519,467	2,339,511
Oklahoma[5]									
Oregon									52,465
Pennsylvania		17,950	119,666	240,057	434,373	602,365	1,049,458	1,724,033	2,906,215
Rhode Island	785	5,894	33,226	58,196	68,825	69,122	83,059	108,830	174,620
South Carolina		5,704	64,000	124,244	249,073	345,591	502,741	594,398	703,708
South Dakota[3]									4,837
Tennessee				1,000	35,691	105,602	422,823	829,210	1,109,801
Texas									604,215
Utah									40,273
Vermont				10,000	85,425	154,465	235,981	291,948	315,098
Virginia[6]	18,731	58,560	231,033	447,016	691,737	807,557	938,261	1,025,227	1,219,630
Washington									11,594
West Virginia[6]					55,873	78,592	136,808	224,537	376,688
Wisconsin								30,945	775,881
Wyoming									
Total[1]	50,368	250,888	1,170,760	2,148,076	3,929,214	5,308,483	9,638,453	17,069,453[2]	31,443,321

[1] All figures prior to 1890 exclude Indians unaffected by the pioneer movement. Figures for 1650 through 1770 include only the British colonies that later became the United States. No areas are included prior to their annexation to the United States. However, many of the figures refer to territories prior to their admission as states. U.S. total includes Alaska from 1880 through 1970 and Hawaii from 1900 through 1970.

[2] U.S. total for 1840 includes 6,100 persons on public ships in service of the United States not credited to any state.

[3] South Dakota figure for 1860 represents entire Dakota Territory. North and South Dakota figures for 1880 are for the parts of Dakota Territory which later constituted the respective states.

1880	1900	1920	1940	1950	1960	1970	1980	1990	2000
1,262,505	1,828,697	2,348,174	2,832,961	3,061,743	3,266,740	3,444,165	3,893,888	4,062,608	4,447,100
33,426	63,592	55,036	72,524	128,643	226,167	302,173	401,851	551,947	626,932
40,440	122,931	334,162	499,261	749,587	1,302,161	1,772,482	2,718,425	3,677,985	5,130,632
802,525	1,311,564	1,752,204	1,949,387	1,909,511	1,786,272	1,923,295	2,286,435	2,362,239	2,673,400
864,694	1,485,053	3,426,861	6,907,387	10,586,223	15,717,204	19,953,134	23,667,565	29,839,250	33,871,648
194,327	539,700	939,629	1,123,296	1,325,089	1,753,947	2,207,259	2,889,735	3,307,912	4,301,261
622,700	908,420	1,380,631	1,709,242	2,007,280	2,535,234	3,032,217	3,107,576	3,295,669	3,405,565
146,608	184,735	223,003	266,505	318,085	446,292	548,104	594,317	668,696	783,600
177,624	278,718	437,571	663,091	802,178	763,956	756,510	638,432	609,909	572,059
269,493	528,542	968,470	1,897,414	2,771,305	4,951,560	6,789,443	9,746,342	13,003,362	15,982,378
1,542,180	2,216,331	2,895,832	3,123,723	3,444,578	3,943,116	4,589,575	5,463,105	6,508,419	8,186,453
	154,001	255,881	422,770	499,794	632,772	769,913	964,691	1,115,274	1,211,537
32,610	161,772	431,866	524,873	588,637	667,191	713,008	944,038	1,011,986	1,293,953
3,077,871	4,821,550	6,485,280	7,897,241	8,712,176	10,081,158	11,113,976	11,426,596	11,466,682	12,419,293
1,978,301	2,516,462	2,930,390	3,427,796	3,934,224	4,662,498	5,193,669	5,490,260	5,564,228	6,080,485
1,624,615	2,231,853	2,404,021	2,538,268	2,621,073	2,757,537	2,825,041	2,913,808	2,787,424	2,926,324
996,096	1,470,495	1,769,257	1,801,028	1,905,299	2,178,611	2,249,071	2,364,236	2,485,600	2,688,418
1,648,690	2,147,174	2,416,630	2,845,627	2,944,806	3,038,156	3,219,311	3,660,257	3,698,969	4,041,769
939,946	1,381,625	1,798,509	2,363,880	2,683,516	3,257,022	3,643,180	4,206,312	4,238,216	4,468,976
648,936	694,466	768,014	847,226	913,774	969,265	993,663	1,125,027	1,233,223	1,274,923
934,943	1,188,044	1,449,661	1,821,244	2,343,001	3,100,689	3,922,399	4,216,975	4,798,622	5,296,486
1,783,085	2,805,346	3,852,356	4,316,721	4,690,514	5,148,578	5,689,170	5,737,037	6,029,051	6,349,097
1,636,937	2,420,982	3,668,412	5,256,106	6,371,766	7,823,194	8,875,083	9,262,078	9,328,784	9,938,444
780,773	1,751,394	2,387,125	2,792,300	2,982,483	3,413,864	3,805,069	4,075,970	4,387,029	4,919,479
1,131,597	1,551,270	1,790,618	2,183,796	2,178,914	2,178,141	2,216,912	2,520,638	2,586,443	2,844,658
2,168,380	3,106,665	3,404,055	3,784,664	3,954,653	4,319,813	4,677,399	4,916,759	5,137,804	5,595,211
39,159	243,329	548,889	559,456	591,024	674,767	694,409	786,690	803,655	902,195
452,402	1,066,300	1,296,372	1,315,834	1,325,510	1,411,330	1,483,791	1,569,825	1,584,617	1,711,263
62,266	42,335	77,407	110,247	160,083	285,278	488,738	800,493	1,206,152	1,998,257
346,991	411,488	443,083	491,524	533,242	606,921	737,681	920,610	1,113,915	1,235,786
1,131,116	1,883,669	3,155,900	4,160,165	4,835,329	6,066,782	7,168,164	7,364,823	7,748,634	8,414,350
119,565	195,310	360,350	531,818	681,187	951,023	1,016,000	1,302,981	1,521,779	1,819,046
5,082,871	7,268,894	10,385,227	13,479,142	14,830,192	16,782,304	18,241,266	17,558,072	18,044,505	18,976,457
1,399,750	1,893,810	2,559,123	3,571,623	4,061,929	4,556,155	5,082,059	5,881,813	6,657,630	8,049,313
36,909	319,146	646,872	641,935	619,636	632,446	617,761	652,717	641,364	642,200
3,198,062	4,157,545	5,759,394	6,907,612	7,946,627	9,706,397	10,652,017	10,797,624	10,887,325	11,353,140
	790,391	2,028,283	2,336,434	2,233,351	2,328,284	2,559,253	3,025,290	3,157,604	3,450,654
174,768	413,536	783,389	1,089,684	1,521,341	1,768,687	2,091,385	2,633,149	2,853,733	3,421,399
4,282,891	6,302,115	8,720,017	9,900,180	10,498,012	11,319,366	11,793,909	11,863,895	11,924,710	12,281,054
276,531	428,556	604,397	713,346	791,896	859,488	949,723	947,154	1,005,984	1,048,319
995,577	1,340,316	1,683,724	1,899,804	2,117,027	2,382,594	2,590,516	3,121,833	3,505,707	4,012,012
98,268	401,570	636,547	642,961	652,740	680,514	666,257	690,768	699,999	754,844
1,542,359	2,020,616	2,337,885	2,915,841	3,291,718	3,567,089	3,924,164	4,591,120	4,896,641	5,689,283
1,591,749	3,048,710	4,663,228	6,414,824	7,711,194	9,579,677	11,196,730	14,229,288	17,059,805	20,851,820
143,963	276,749	449,396	550,310	688,862	890,627	1,059,273	1,461,037	1,727,784	2,233,169
332,286	343,641	352,428	359,231	377,747	389,881	444,732	551,456	564,964	608,827
1,512,565	1,854,184	2,309,187	2,677,773	3,318,680	3,966,949	4,648,494	5,346,818	6,216,568	7,078,515
75,116	518,103	1,356,621	1,736,191	2,378,963	2,853,214	3,409,169	4,132,180	4,887,941	5,894,121
618,457	958,800	1,463,701	1,901,974	2,005,552	1,860,421	1,744,237	1,950,279	1,801,625	1,808,344
1,315,497	2,069,042	2,632,067	3,137,587	3,434,575	3,951,777	4,417,933	4,705,521	4,906,745	5,363,675
20,789	92,531	194,402	250,742	290,529	330,066	332,416	469,557	455,975	493,782
50,189,209	76,212,168	106,021,537	132,164,569	151,325,798	179,323,175	203,235,298	226,547,346	249,632,692	281,421,906

[4]Maine figures for 1770 through 1800 are for that area of Massachusetts which became the state of Maine in 1820. Massachusetts figures exclude Maine from 1770 through 1800, but include it from 1650 through 1750. Massachusetts figure for 1650 also includes population of Plymouth (1,566), a separate colony until 1691.

[5]Oklahoma figure for 1900 includes population of Indian Territory (392,060).

[6]West Virginia figures for 1790 through 1860 are for that area of Virginia which became West Virginia in 1863. These figures are excluded from the figures for Virginia from 1790 through 1860.

Facts About the States

State	Admission to the Union date (order)	Capital	Area in sq.mi. (rank in area)	Nickname	Postal Abbreviation
Alabama	1819 (22)	Montgomery	50,744 (28)	Heart of Dixie	AL
Alaska	1959 (49)	Juneau	571,951 (1)	Last Frontier	AK
Arizona	1912 (48)	Phoenix	113,635 (6)	Grand Canyon State	AZ
Arkansas	1836 (25)	Little Rock	52,068 (27)	Natural State	AR
California	1850 (31)	Sacramento	155,959 (3)	Golden State	CA
Colorado	1876 (38)	Denver	103,718 (8)	Centennial State	CO
Connecticut	1788 (5)	Hartford	4,845 (48)	Constitution State	CT
Delaware	1787 (1)	Dover	1,954 (49)	First State	DE
Florida	1845 (27)	Tallahassee	53,927 (26)	Sunshine State	FL
Georgia	1788 (4)	Atlanta	57,906 (21)	Peach State	GA
Hawaii	1959 (50)	Honolulu	6,423 (47)	Aloha State	HI
Idaho	1890 (43)	Boise	82,747 (11)	Gem State	ID
Illinois	1818 (21)	Springfield	55,584 (24)	Land of Lincoln	IL
Indiana	1816 (19)	Indianapolis	35,867 (38)	Hoosier State	IN
Iowa	1846 (29)	Des Moines	55,869 (23)	Hawkeye State	IA
Kansas	1861 (34)	Topeka	81,815 (13)	Sunflower State	KS
Kentucky	1792 (15)	Frankfort	39,728 (36)	Bluegrass State	KY
Louisiana	1812 (18)	Baton Rouge	43,562 (33)	Pelican State	LA
Maine	1820 (23)	Augusta	30,862 (39)	Pine Tree State	ME
Maryland	1788 (7)	Annapolis	9,774 (42)	Old Line State	MD
Massachusetts	1788 (6)	Boston	7,840 (45)	Bay State	MA
Michigan	1837 (26)	Lansing	56,804 (22)	Wolverine State	MI
Minnesota	1858 (32)	St. Paul	79,610 (14)	North Star State	MN
Mississippi	1817 (20)	Jackson	46,907 (31)	Magnolia State	MS
Missouri	1821 (24)	Jefferson City	68,886 (18)	Show Me State	MO

State	Admission to the Union date (order)	Capital	Area in sq.mi. (rank in area)	Nickname	Postal Abbreviation
Montana	1889 (41)	Helena	145,552 (4)	Treasure State	MT
Nebraska	1867 (37)	Lincoln	76,872 (15)	Cornhusker State	NE
Nevada	1864 (36)	Carson City	109,826 (7)	Silver State	NV
New Hampshire	1788 (9)	Concord	8,968 (44)	Granite State	NH
New Jersey	1787 (3)	Trenton	7,417 (46)	Garden State	NJ
New Mexico	1912 (47)	Santa Fe	121,356 (5)	Land of Enchantment	NM
New York	1788 (11)	Albany	47,214 (30)	Empire State	NY
North Carolina	1789 (12)	Raleigh	48,711 (29)	Tar Heel State	NC
North Dakota	1889 (39)	Bismarck	68,976 (17)	Peace Garden State	ND
Ohio	1803 (17)	Columbus	40,948 (35)	Buckeye State	OH
Oklahoma	1907 (46)	Oklahoma City	68,667 (19)	Sooner State	OK
Oregon	1859 (33)	Salem	95,997 (10)	Beaver State	OR
Pennsylvania	1787 (2)	Harrisburg	44,817 (32)	Keystone State	PA
Rhode Island	1790 (13)	Providence	1,045 (50)	Ocean State	RI
South Carolina	1788 (8)	Columbia	30,109 (40)	Palmetto State	SC
South Dakota	1889 (40)	Pierre	75,885 (16)	Mount Rushmore State	SD
Tennessee	1796 (16)	Nashville	41,217 (34)	Volunteer State	TN
Texas	1845 (28)	Austin	261,797 (2)	Lone Star State	TX
Utah	1896 (45)	Salt Lake City	82,144 (12)	Beehive State	UT
Vermont	1791 (14)	Montpelier	9,250 (43)	Green Mountain State	VT
Virginia	1788 (10)	Richmond	39,594 (37)	Old Dominion	VA
Washington	1889 (42)	Olympia	66,544 (20)	Evergreen State	WA
West Virginia	1863 (35)	Charleston	24,078 (41)	Mountain State	WV
Wisconsin	1848 (30)	Madison	54,310 (25)	Badger State	WI
Wyoming	1890 (44)	Cheyenne	97,100 (9)	Equality State	WY

In addition to place names that appear on the maps in this atlas, the Index also lists names of people, groups, events, and other topics related to American history. It provides explanatory information, such as dates, identifications, and geographic locations for many entries. When appropriate, entries are cross-referenced to related topics.

The Index lists boldfaced page numbers on which each entry appears. A small letter beside a page number identifies a specific map on the page on which the entry appears. Postal abbreviations are used for state names.

The following abbreviations also are used:

Ft.	Fort	St.	Saint
g	graph	t	table
Is.	Islands	terr.	territory
p	photograph	U.S.	United States
pop.	population		